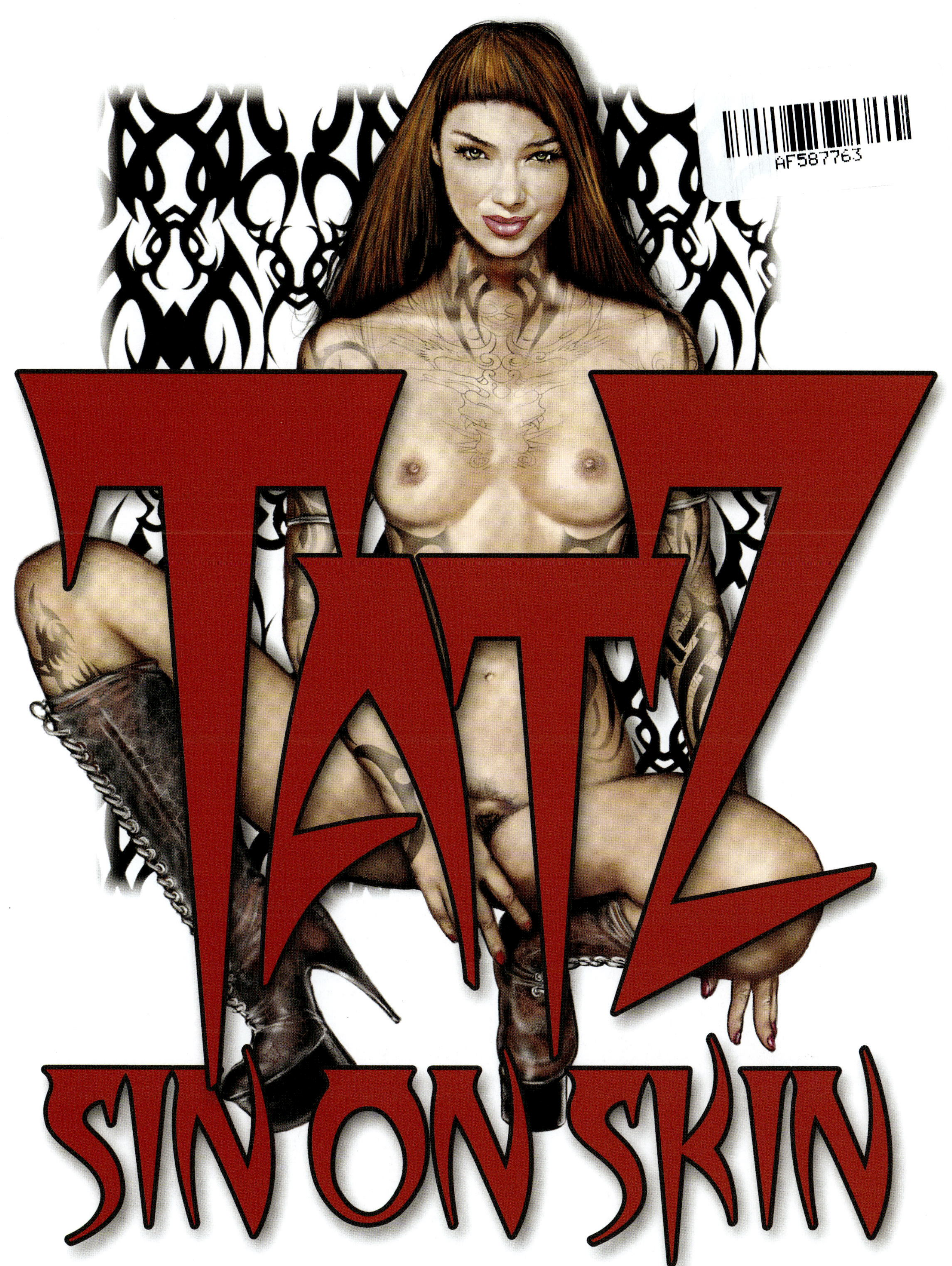

BY STEFANO MAZZOTTI & VINCENZO SILVESTRONI WITH SARA FERRI

AN SQP PRESENTATION

SQP Inc - PO Box 248 - Columbus, NJ 08022 - On the web - www.sqpinc.com - Sal Quartuccio and Bob Keenan - Publishers

NAGASAKA MIDORI

My face reflects every battle I have fought.
I have stared down every peril, armed with my swords and safe in my armor.
The design I choose to ornament my legs and arms celebrate each battle I have won.
Every single one.
But now I'm not sure of my pure samurai spirit.
I can not recognize my thoughts.
My belly should be quartered.
I have no place for another tattoo.
I need that place to tell myself about my weakness.
Love is the enemy.
It cuts too deep.

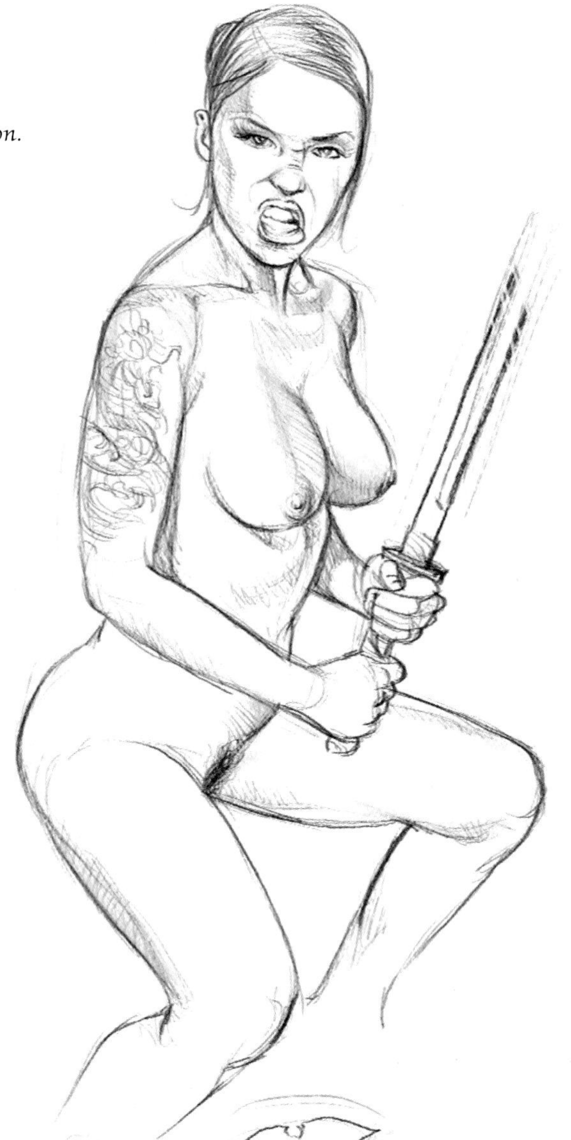

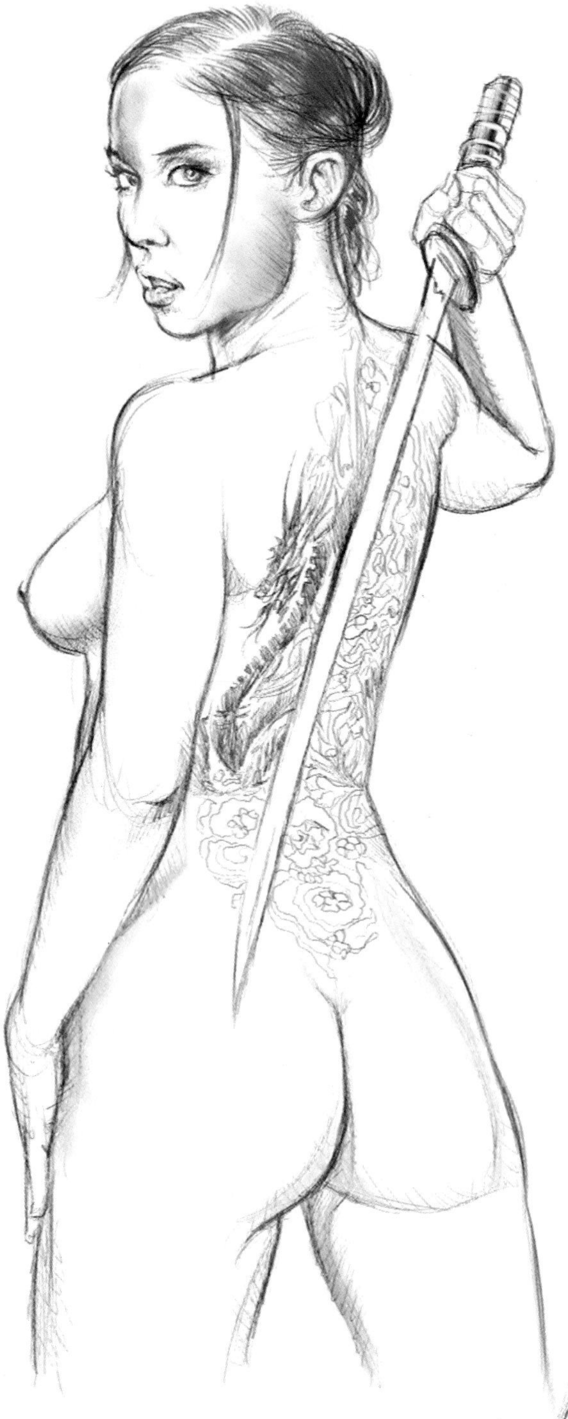

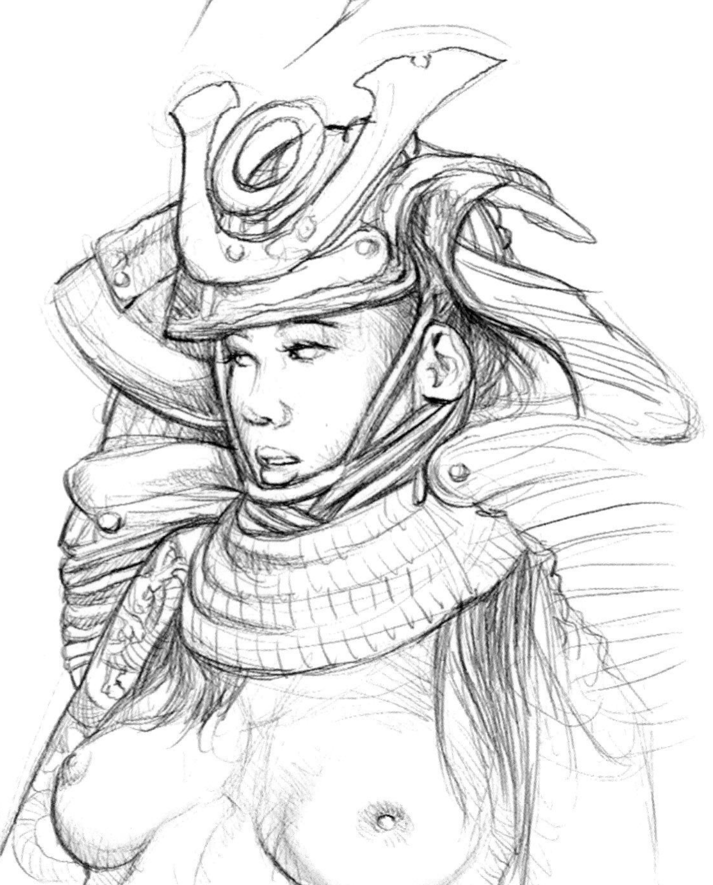

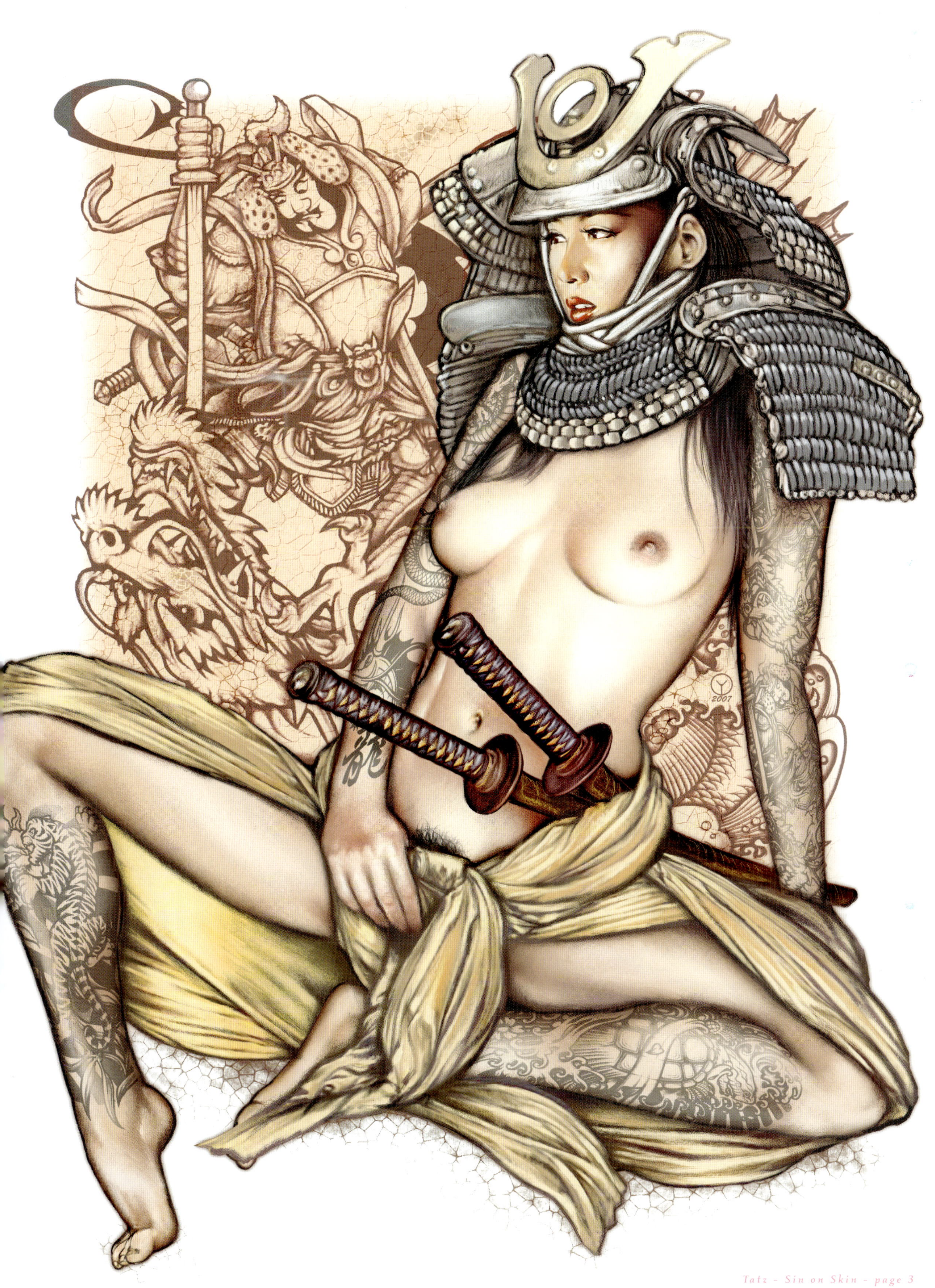

AARA JOUNGLUSTEN

*I came in from the wilderness, in a forest of northern Scandinavia.
My father was of Japanese descent, but you'd never believe it by looking at me.
Anyway, all his stories of ghosts and demons and dragons thrilled me when I was young.
Now that I am a woman, I've decided to cover my body with the images I saw when
I was that child in bed, trying to stay warm in those long dark polar nights.
All the beasts of the forest are now tattooed on my skin.
They will protect me when I meet the man of my dreams.*

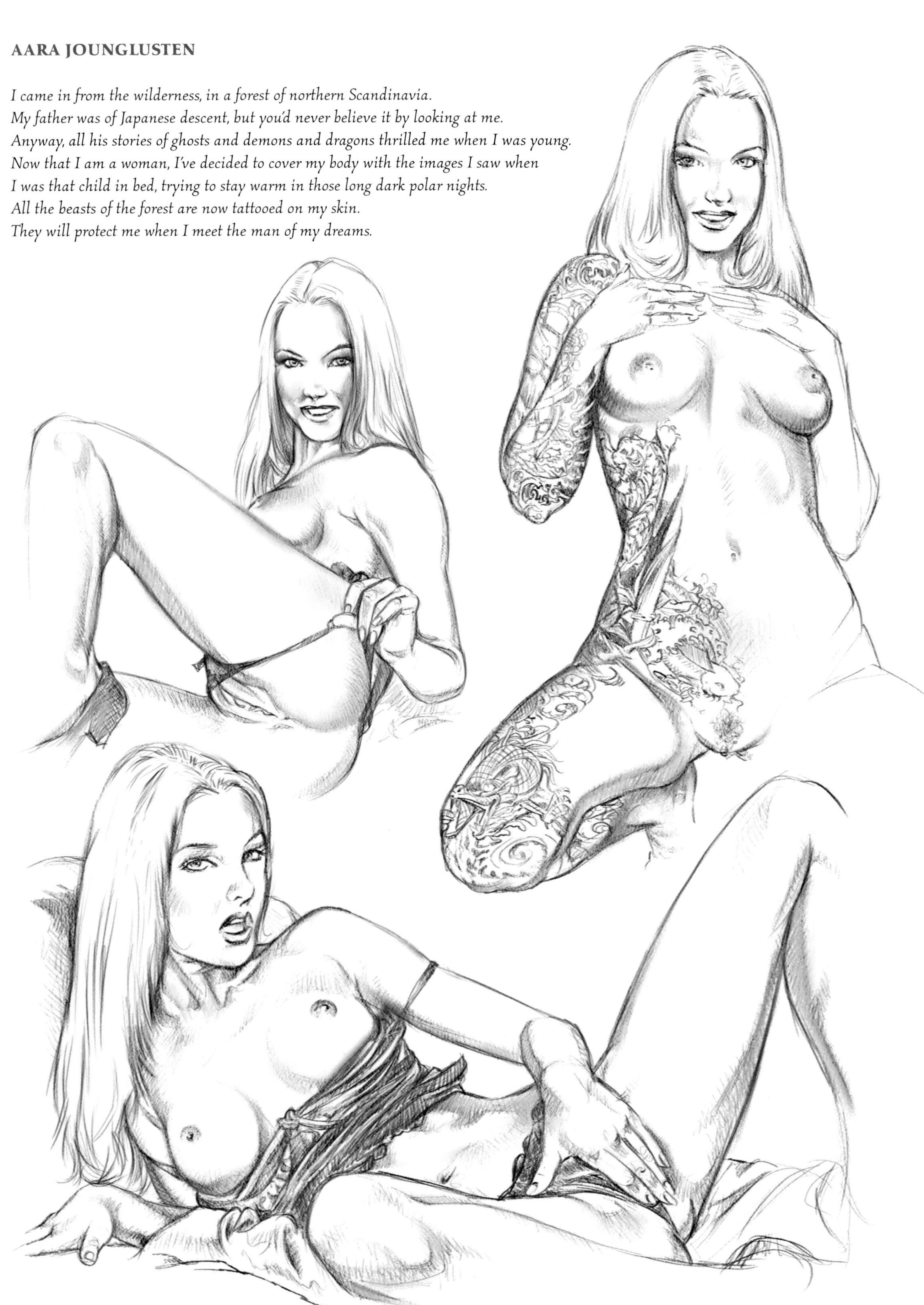

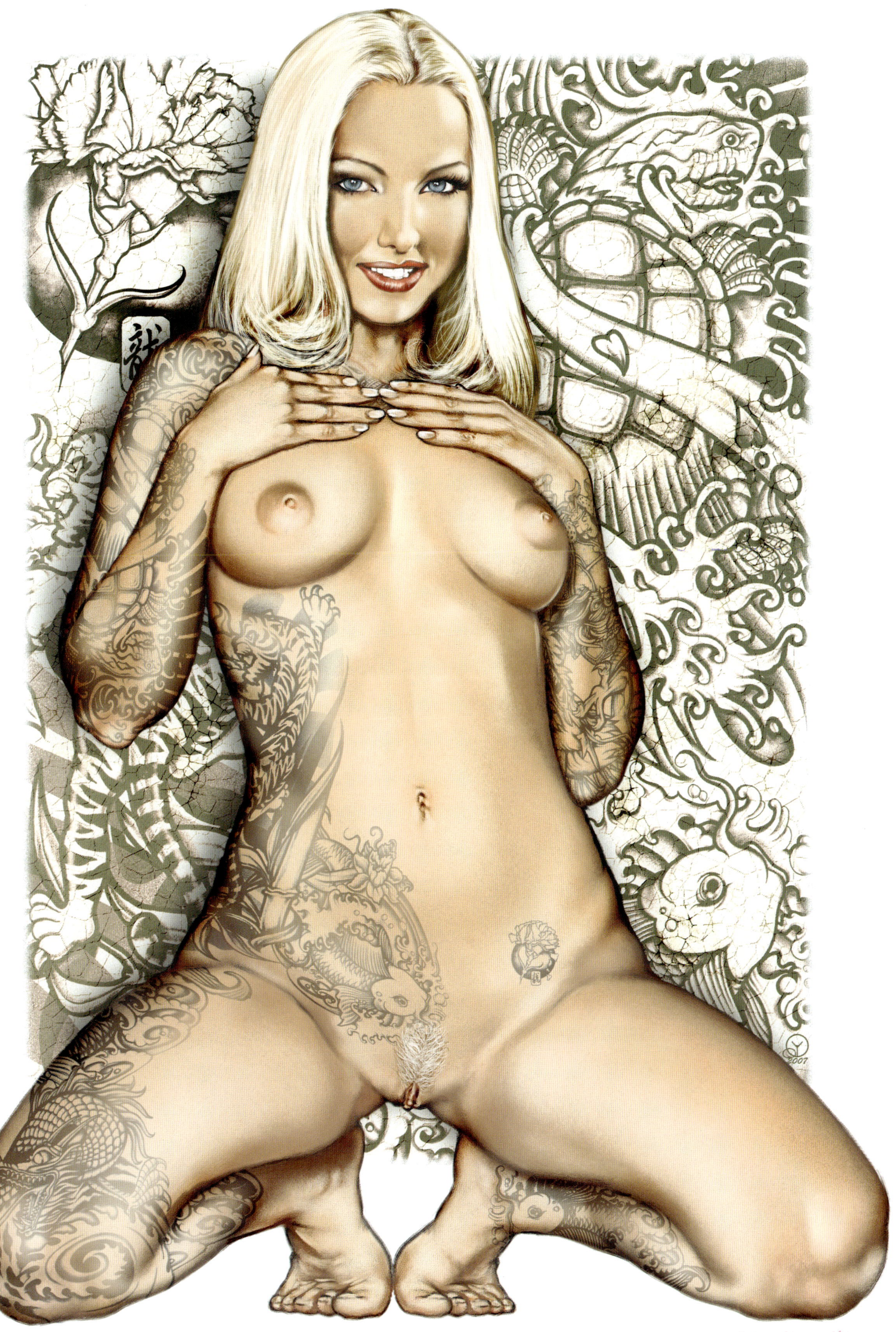

AISTEMAS MIDORI

I am really more shy than my sister Nagasaka.
That's why I don't like to be in the center of the stage like her.
But we both love tattoos. Only, you see, I don't want to have my feet naked.
Don't know why. Maybe because I'm shy.
You see, it is almost Springtime, I'm at home and I can't get my feet warm.
They are naked and cold.
But when Summer comes, I can't walk the streets with my socks on.
And I don't want to have my feet naked, so I tattooed them.
They will never be naked again!
Now I'm waiting for my man.
Then my feet will never be cold again!

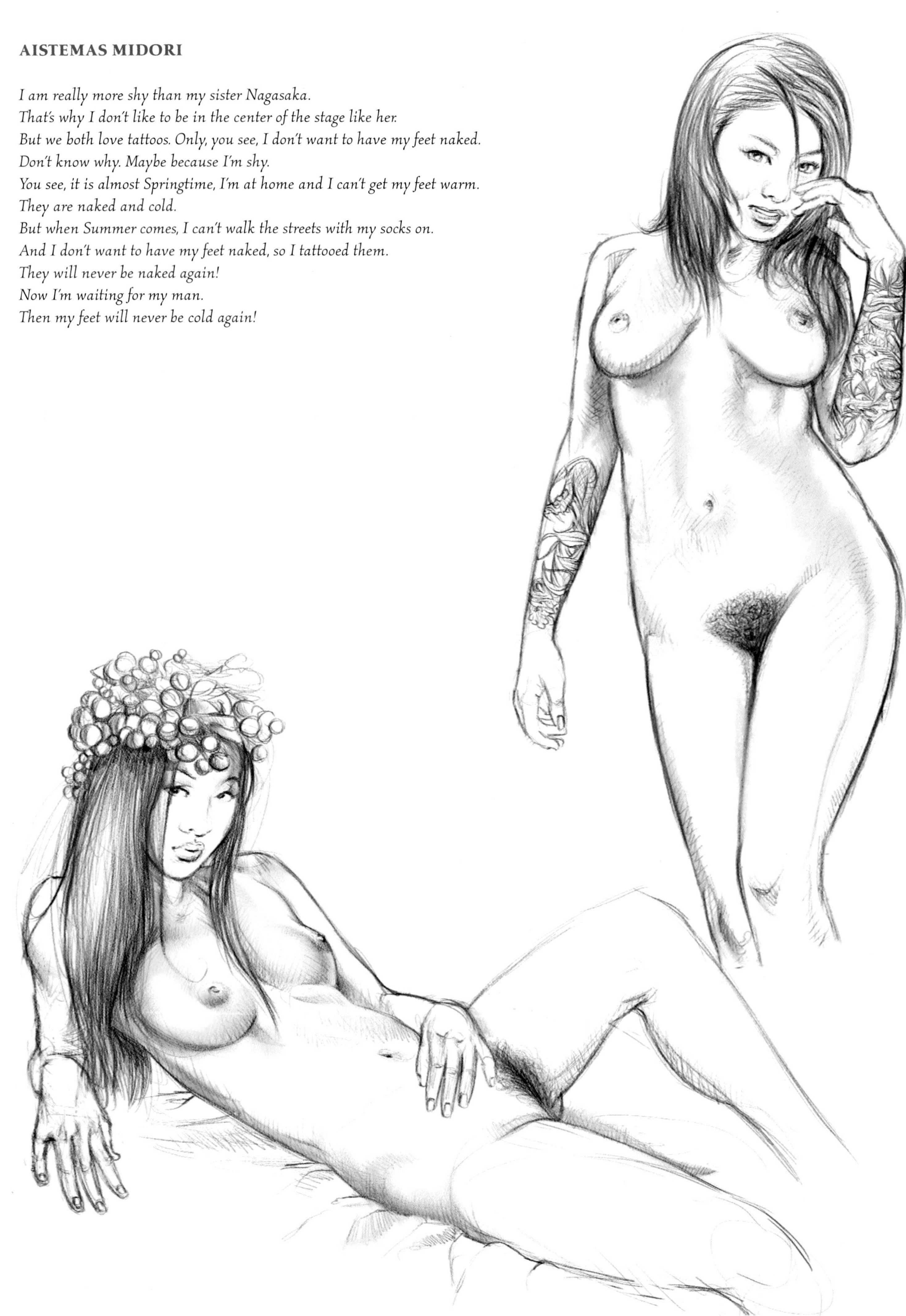

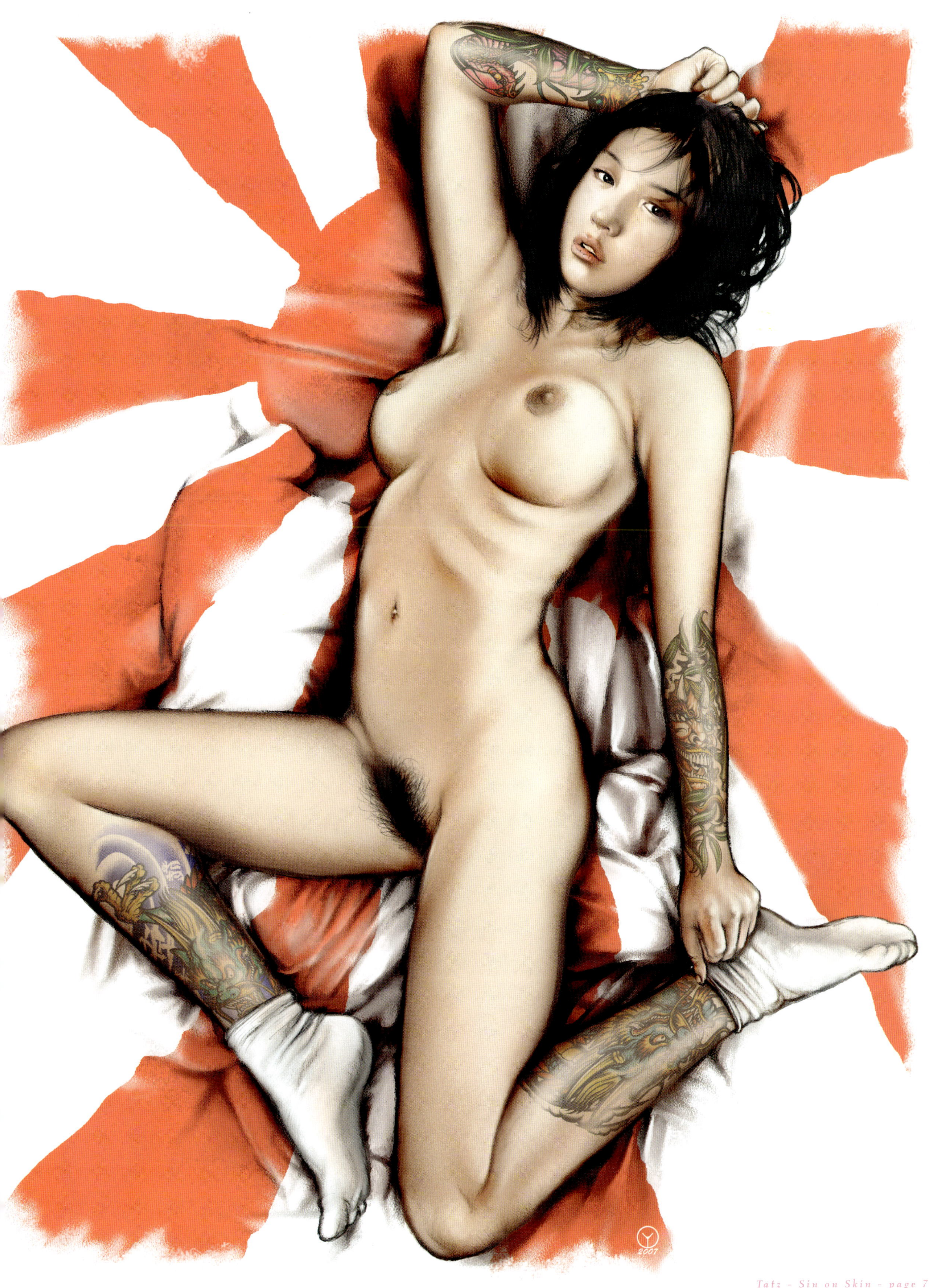

PAULA JEANS

I've always loved roses.
And I've always loved men.
When I was 29 I decided to have a rose tattooed on my body for every man who's known me. And known my pussy.
So I went to the tattoo shop and I talked with the top guy there.
I told him about Mark, Vincent, Stephen (the strangest one), Paul, Henry and all the other lovers I had. All the other lovers that had me.
He began to work with his electric pen and he gave me a garden of 26 roses.
I had asked for 25, but he smiled and said that one was for him.
I nodded in agreement, and tipped the gardener for his fine work.

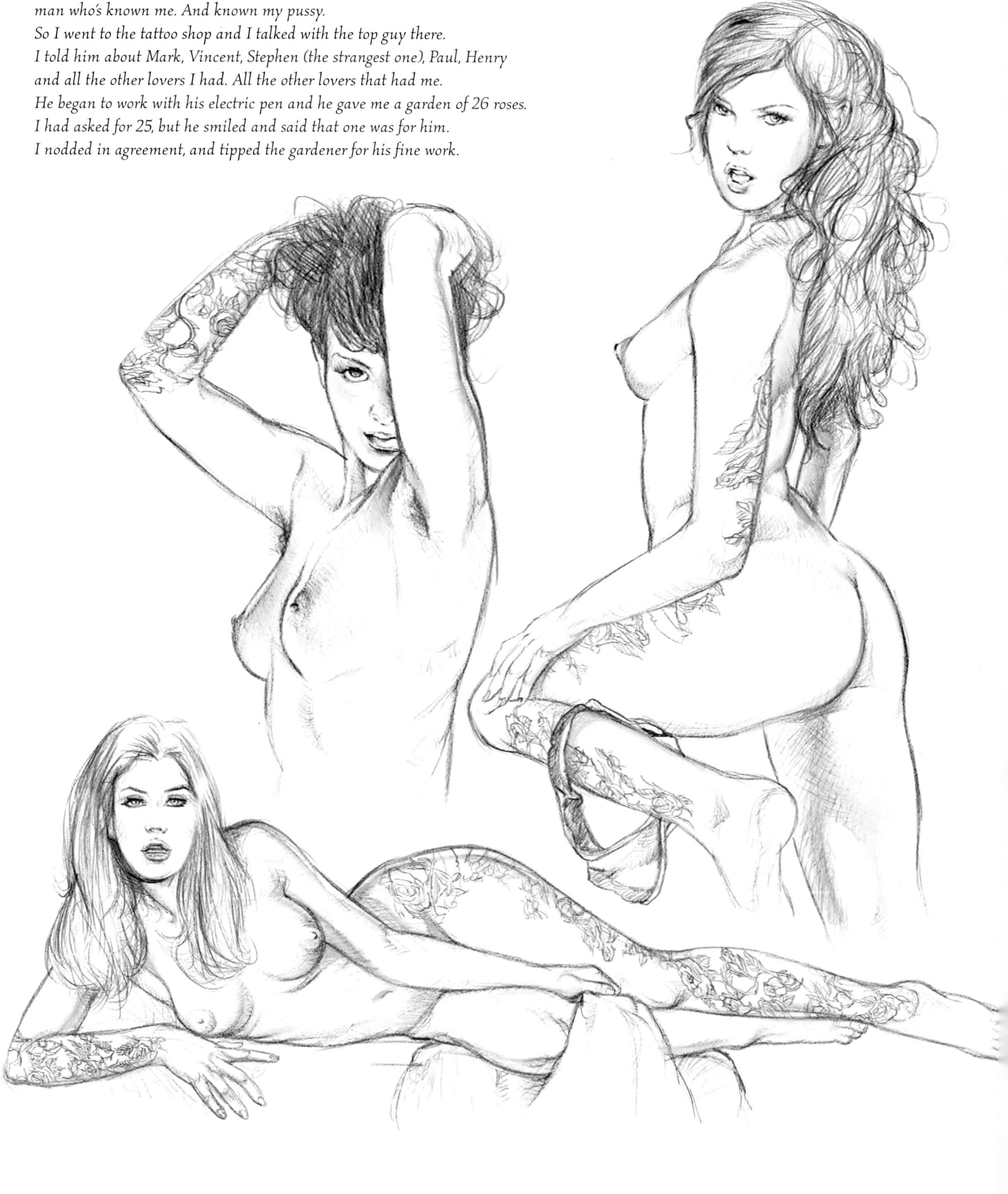

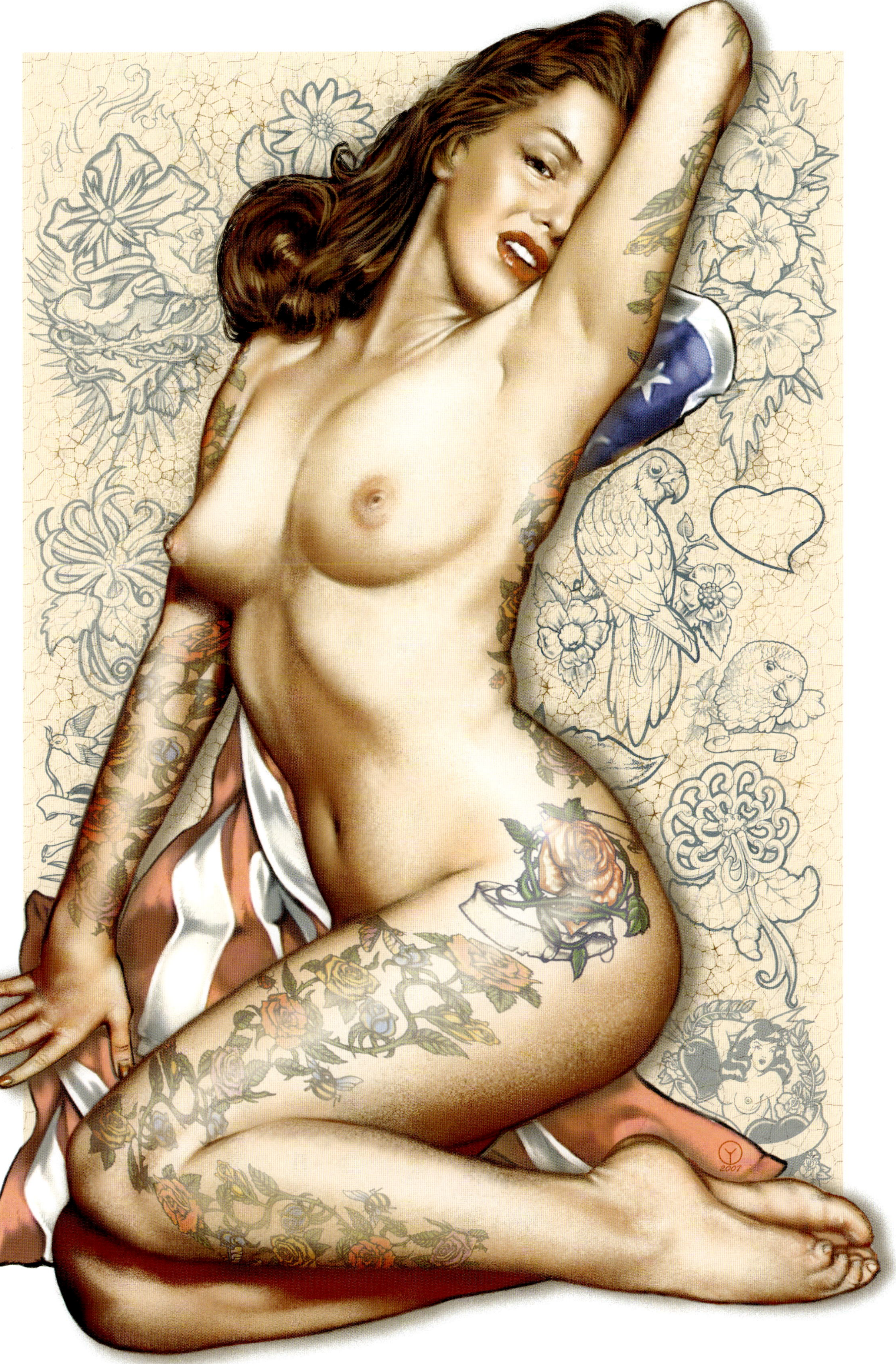

SURELY SUN

Surely, I like the sun.
Surely, I'm a little shy.
Surely, I have my arms and my legs tattooed like a dock worker.
Surely, I was 20 in 1960.
Surely, I was ahead of my time!

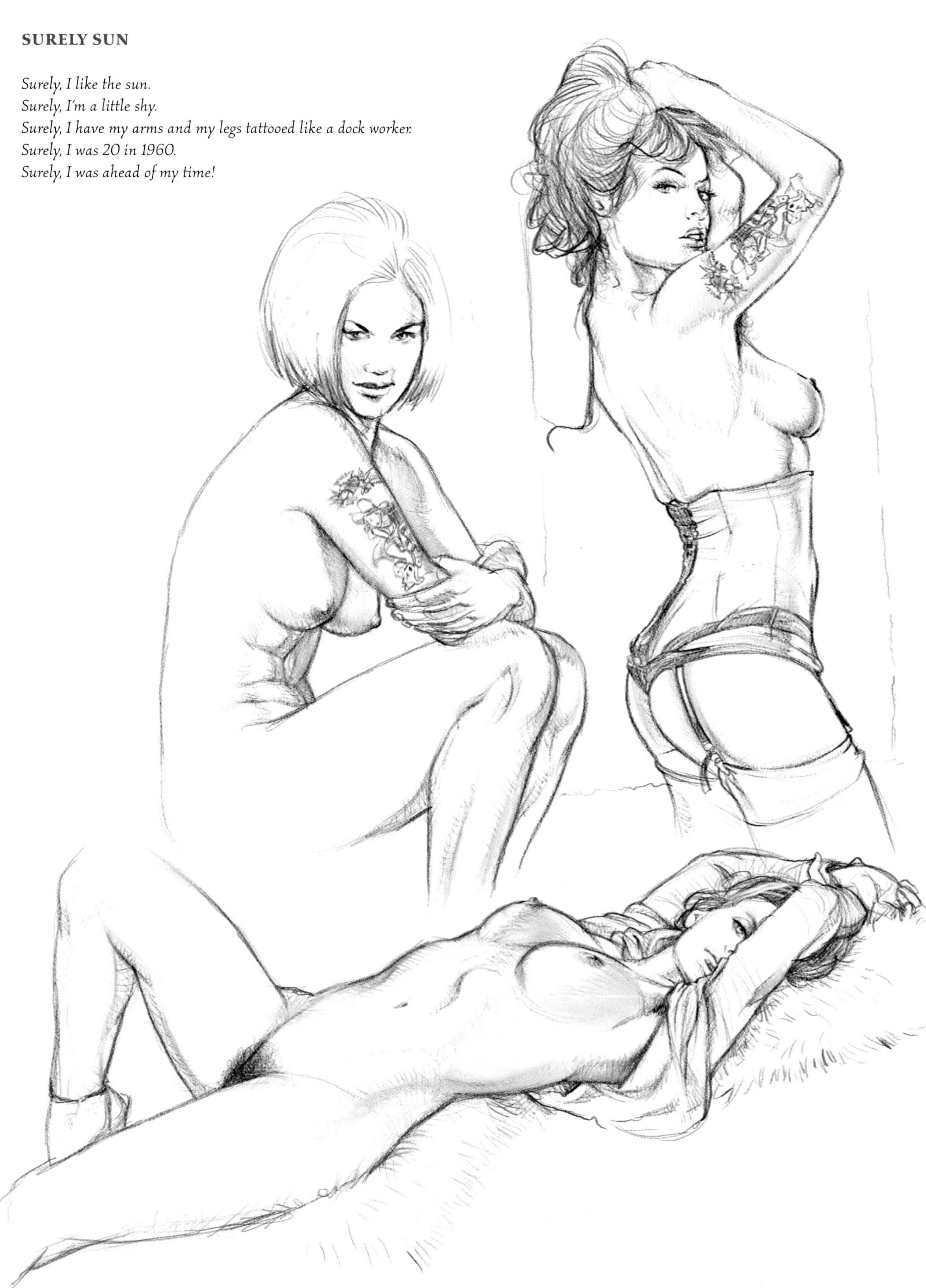

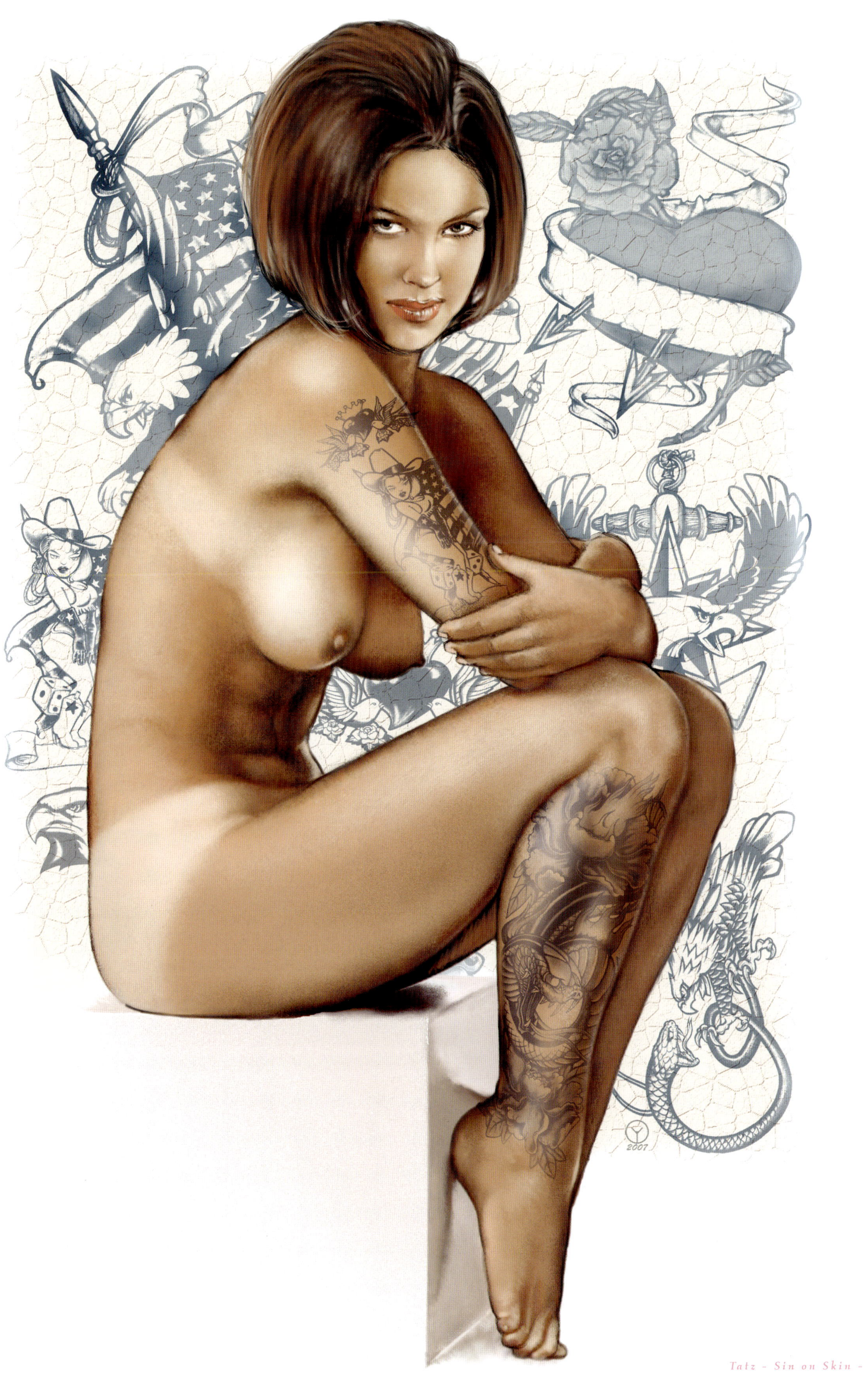
2007

ATITIOKU TOSHITAKE

For a Japanese girl, I have very big tits, like melons. That's not fair.
Japanese girls must have lovely firm lemons.
But my father, a sailor, was Italian, from the north of that country.
That's why I have a Japanese name and Italian tits.
From the time I was a child I was fascinated by the drawings my father had on
his arms; dragons, butterflies, skulls and other images.
Whenever I think of him, I don't see his face as much as I remember those arms!
So one day, I thought I would distract people from staring at my chest
if I had my arms covered in tattoos – like my father!
Now I have twice as many people staring at me.
I must learn to enjoy being different.

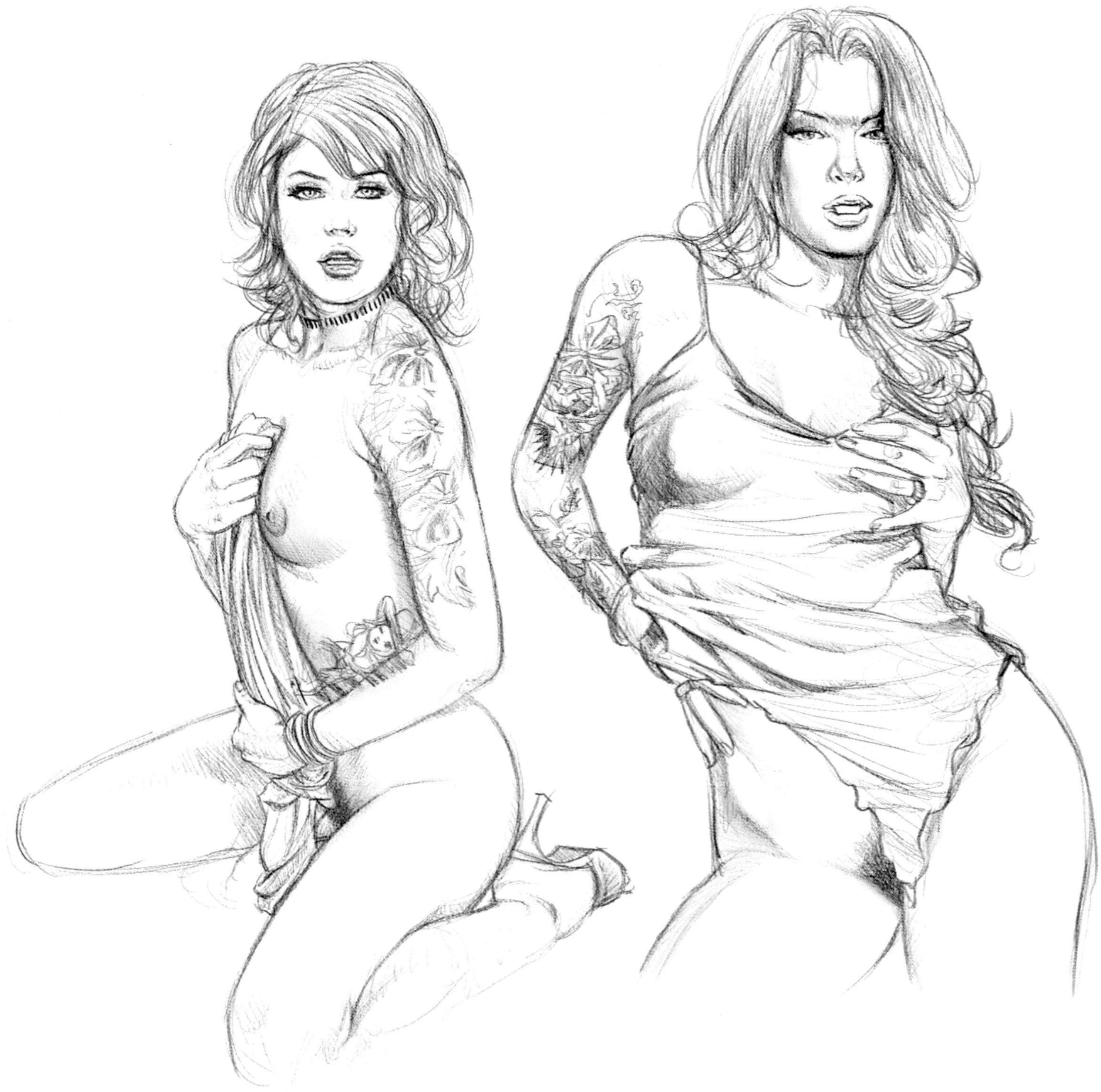

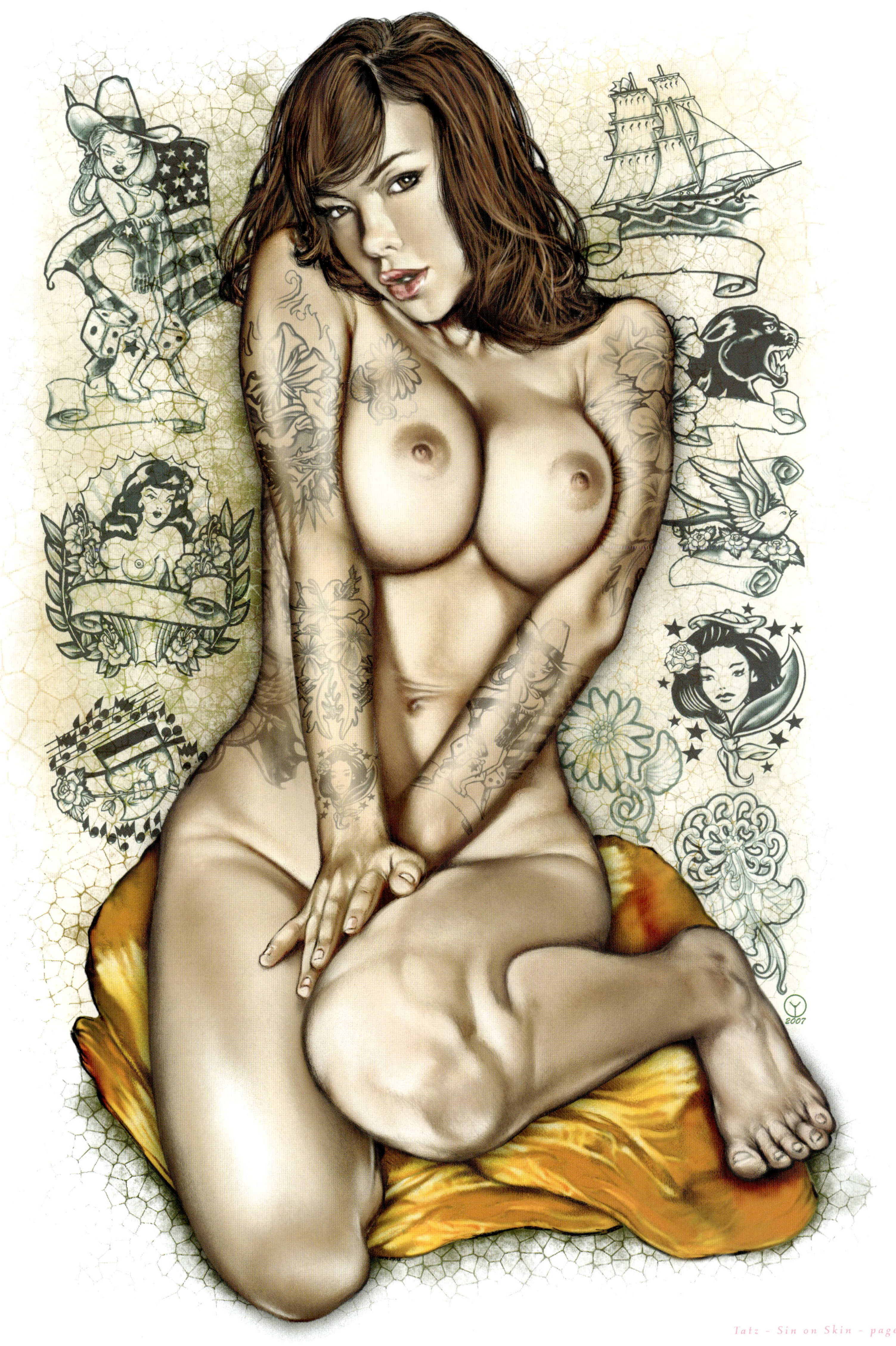

SOLE BALDAZZI

Living in California, everyday is a sunny day.
You have all the road to Vegas to run until you stop.
My pop's Italian and gave me my name, which means "sun" , so yeah, I'm a sunny girl.
I like to meet guys when the sun is high in the sky.
I like to get fucked while feeling the broiling heat shimmer off the black top.
I like the nasty tickle of sweat as it rolls down the crack of my ass.
I want the guy who fucks me to think he's had his dick in the center of the sun!
That's sun worship, baby!
That's Sole worship!

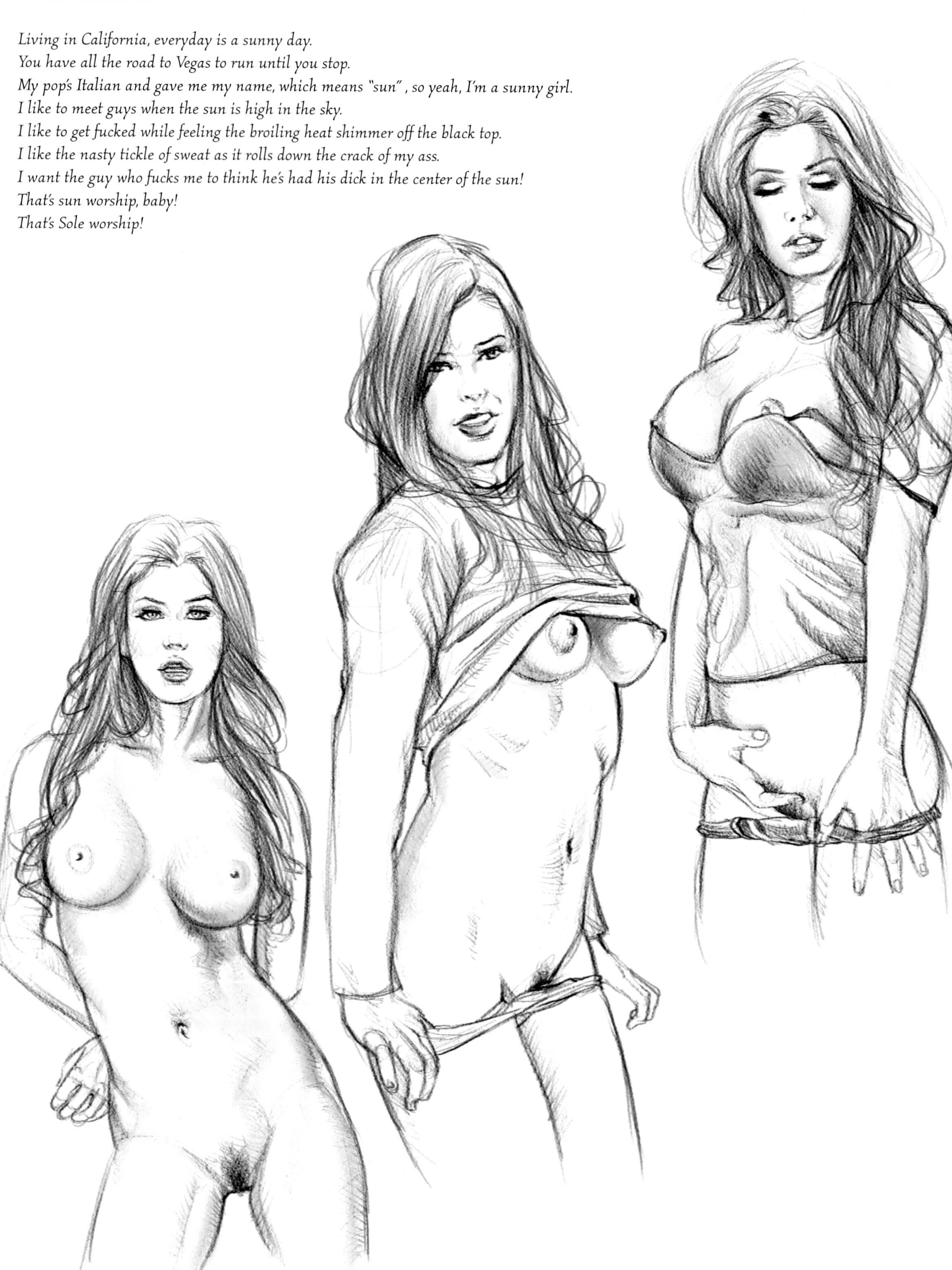

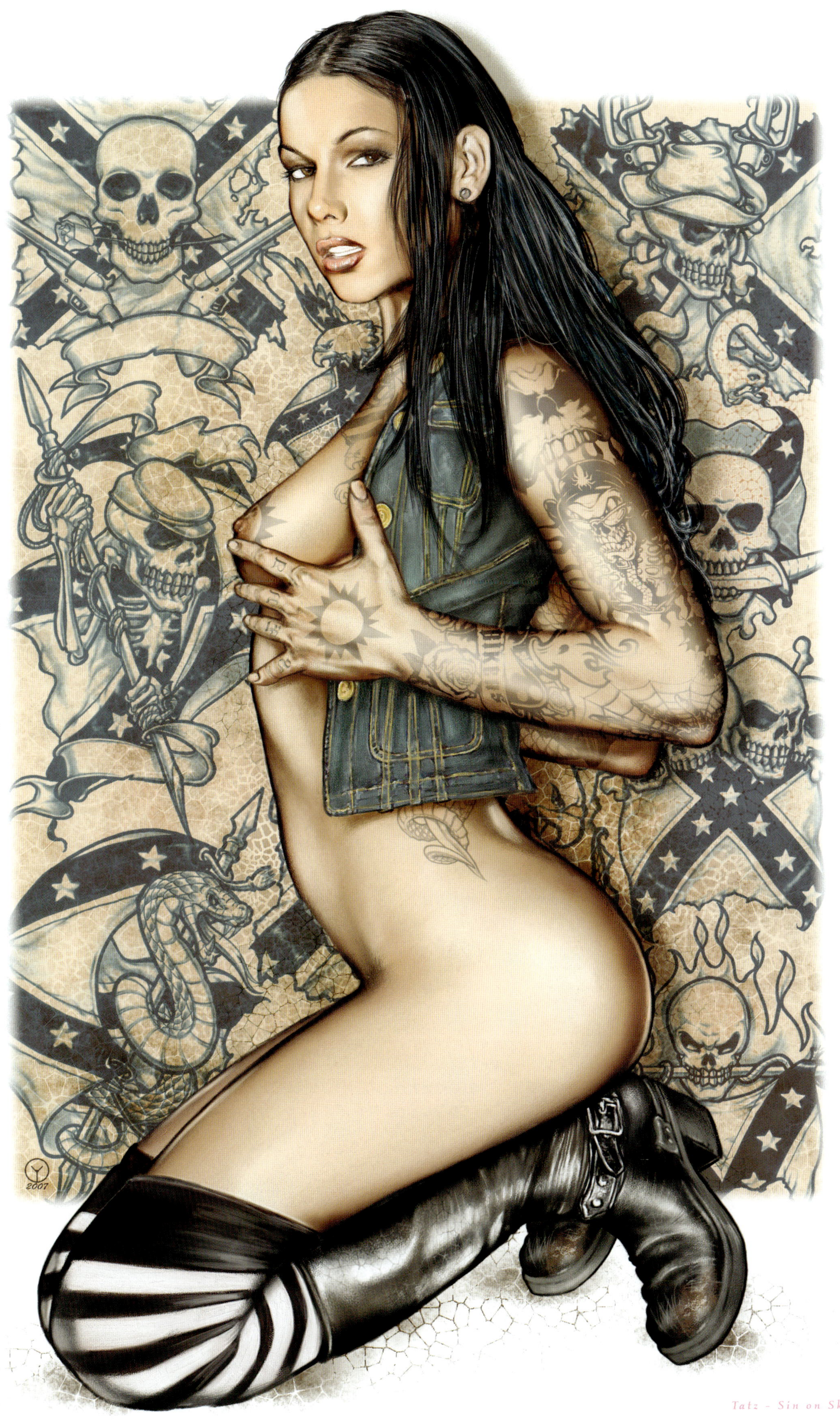

JANINE ARLAZZI

I have been in the joint four times.
Stupid shit, not worth talking about.
Everytime I was in, I get some fresh ink.
Guess it was my way of fitting in, while telling the world to fuck off.
Now I'm out (and plan to stay out), and these prison tats are just not me anymore.
I'd get them lasered, but that costs too much.
I've decided to get them covered with some professional ink.
Turns out, my girl, the tattoo artist I live with, does really nice work!

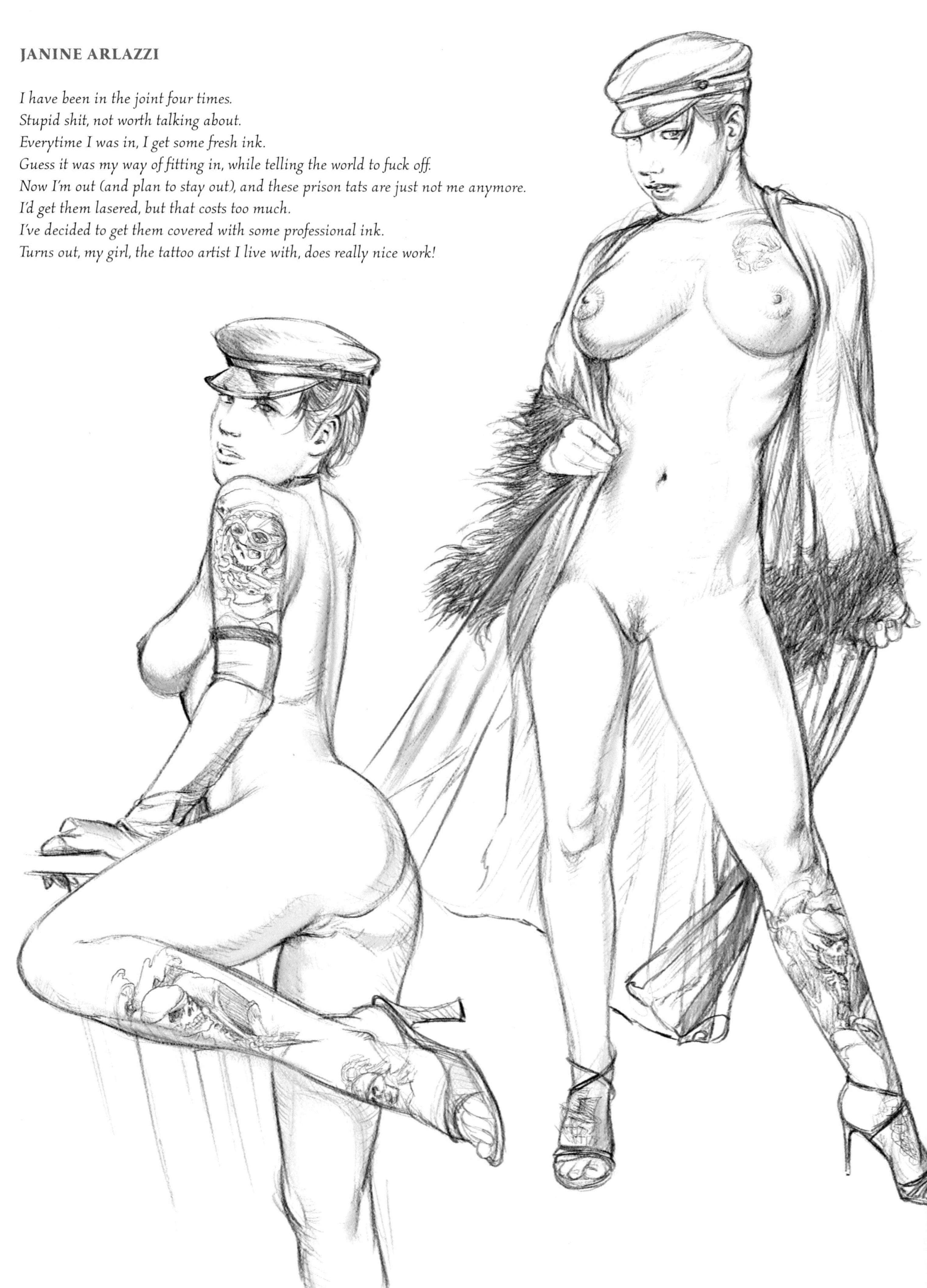

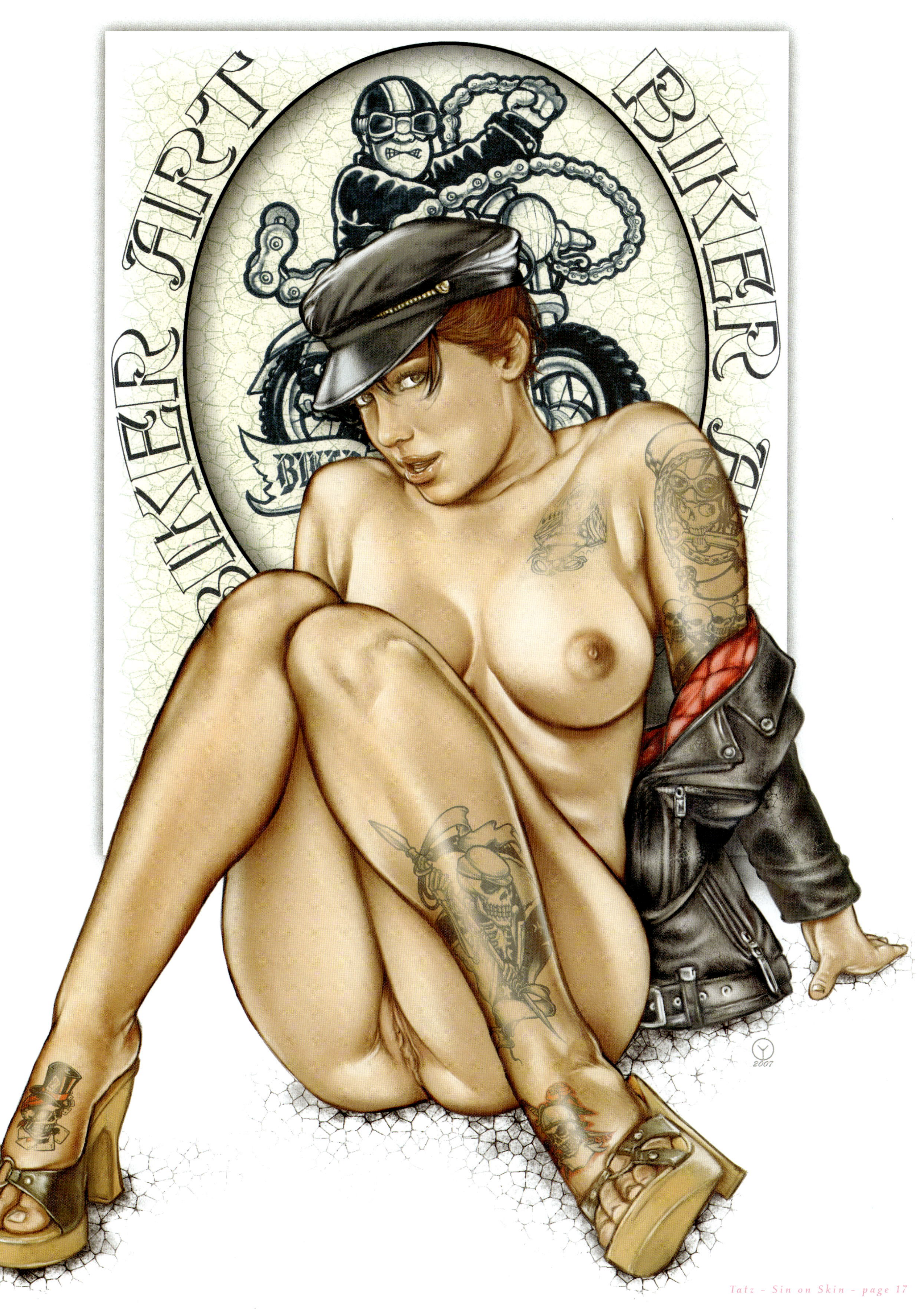
BIKER ART
BIKER
2007

NORA MILLER

It all started with a dare.
Got a kick-ass skull on my arm. Kinda liked it.
Then a dragon on my shoulder, kinda looking out for me.
Then another dragon, standin' guard outside the fuzzy gates.
Who goes there?! Should get another one for my ass!
I've been markin' this map of mine for a few years now.
No tellin' where I'll end up, but at least I'll have a record of the trip!

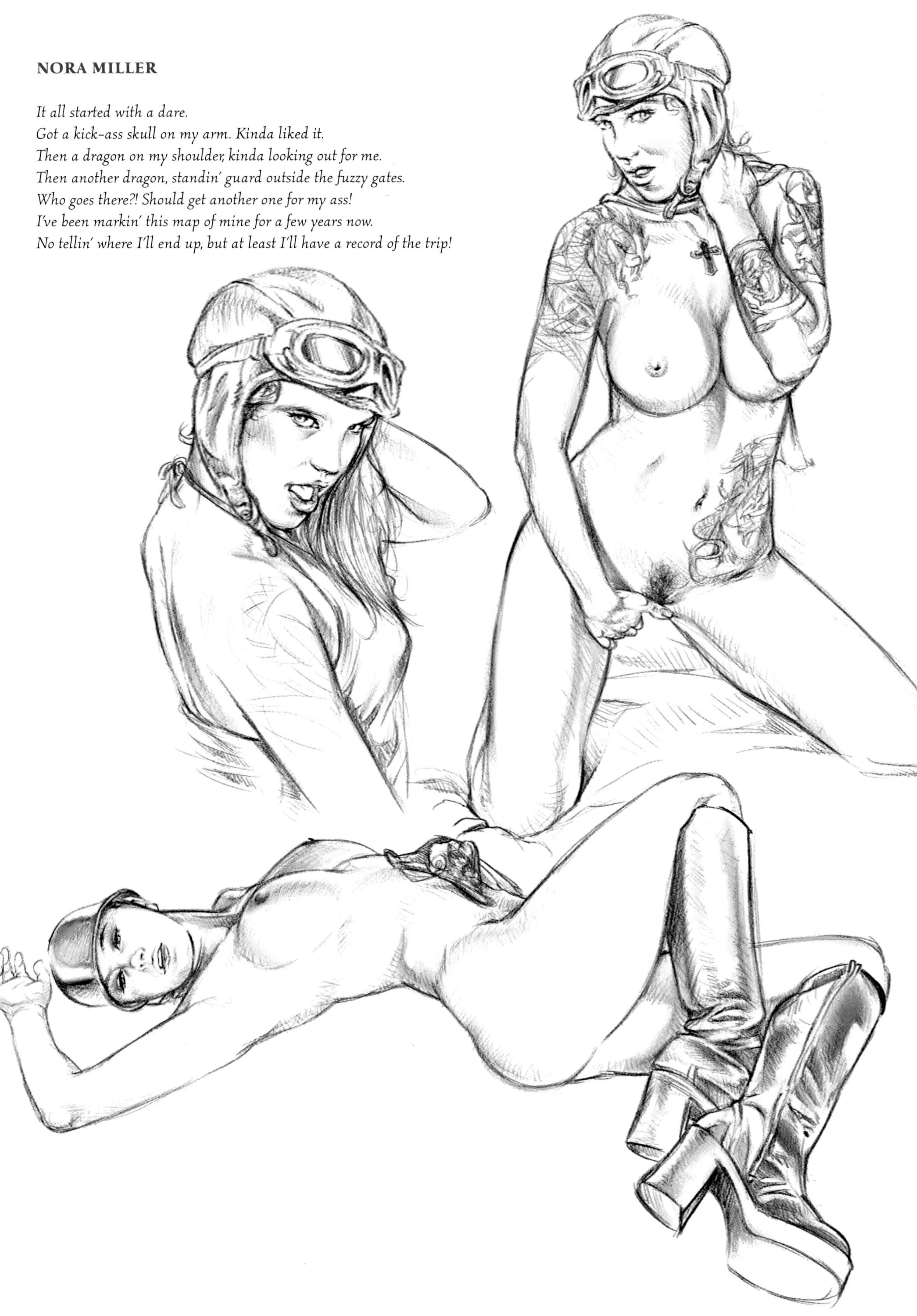

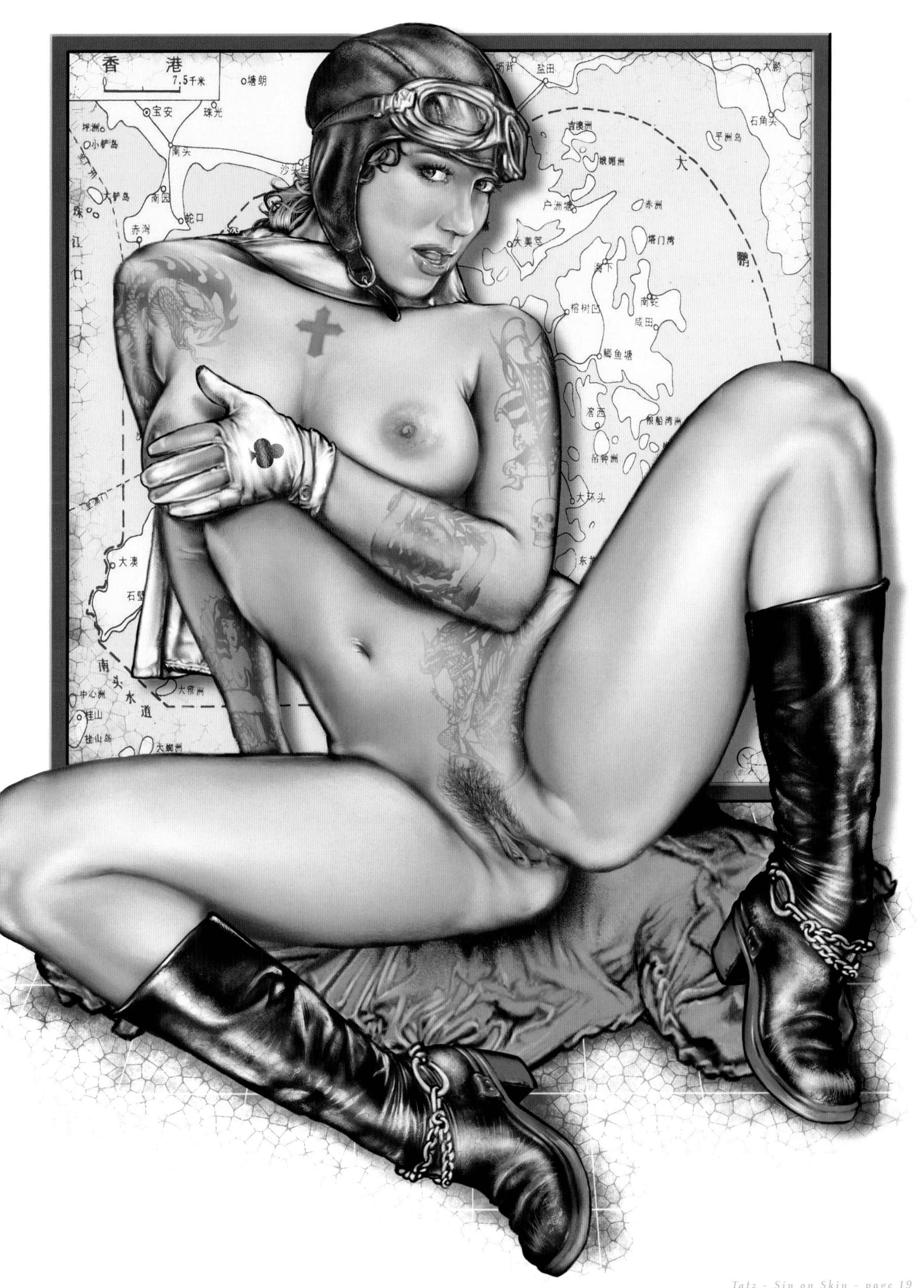
香港
7.5千米
塘朗
宝安
珠光
坪洲
小铲岛
南头
大铲岛
南园
蛇口
赤湾
盐田
大鹏
石角头
平洲岛
赤洲
塔门洲
海下
南蛇
咸田
吊钟洲
大澳
石壁
中心洲
桂山
桂山岛

JEAN DELAGROTE, born JOHN DELLA GROTTA

You know that organized crime is not the easiest life to get out of.
Here I was, this Italian kid born in New Zealand, and growing up, a huge fan of the native culture. I was totally into it – at least the surface stuff – especially the tattoos! Got myself fully inked – old school with traditional methods – no pussy modern electric needle for me!
Looked fuckin' cool!
Made me feel alive!
Then my cousin Frankie got me involved in some really dark shit – drugs, guns, smuggling, protection – the whole nine yards.
Hey, I was young, dumb, and full of cum – what did I know?
Got pinched in the States, and the Feds gave me an out.
Connect some dots for them, and they'd give me a whole new identity.
Man, they weren't kidding!
I got some tits, a pussy, some hormones...
Looked fuckin' cool!
Made me feel alive!
If you ever find yourself in San Francisco, check out "Devil Dolls" downtown. I'm usually on the pole from 9 to midnight.
But you didn't hear that from "Johnny Grotts"!

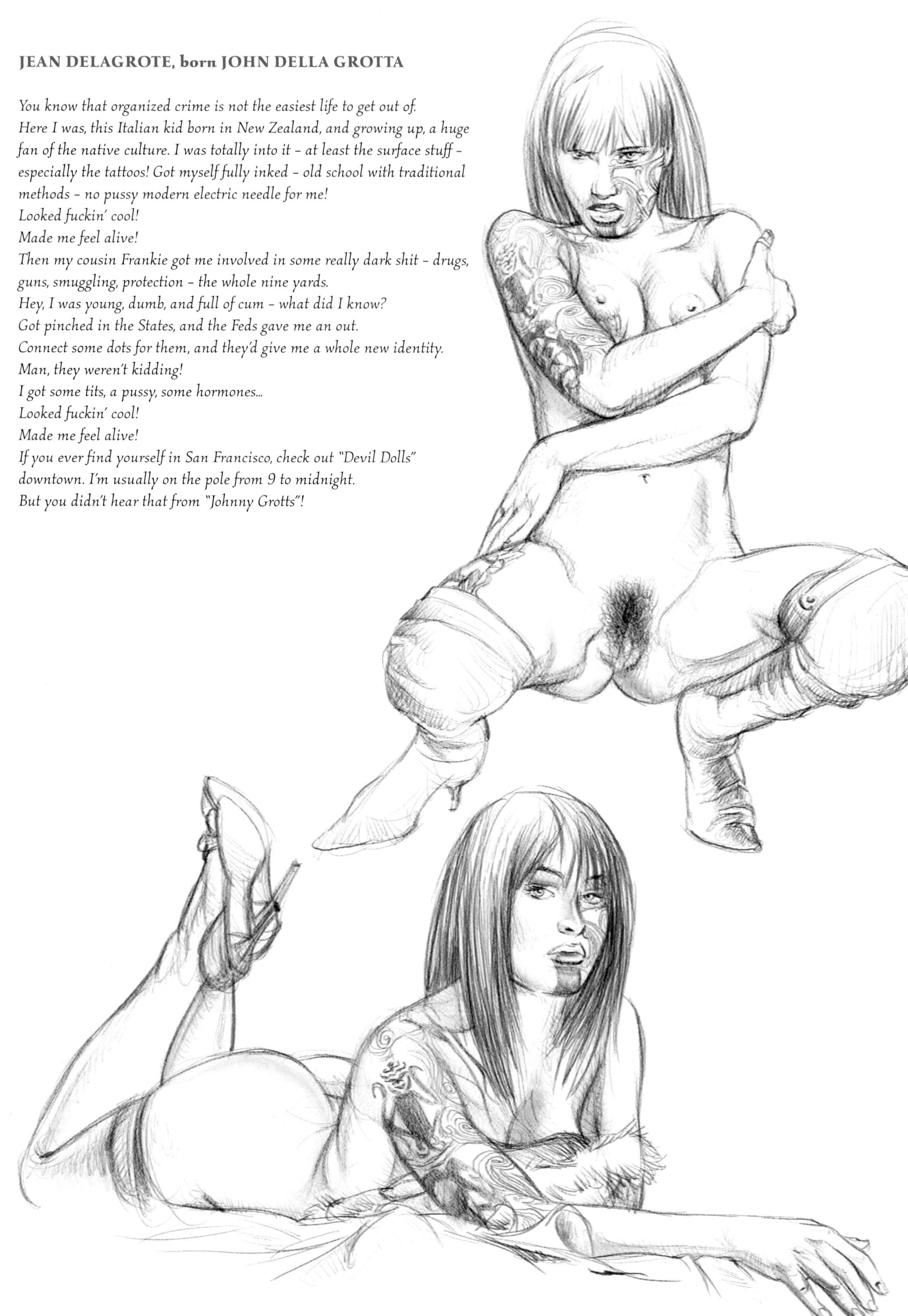

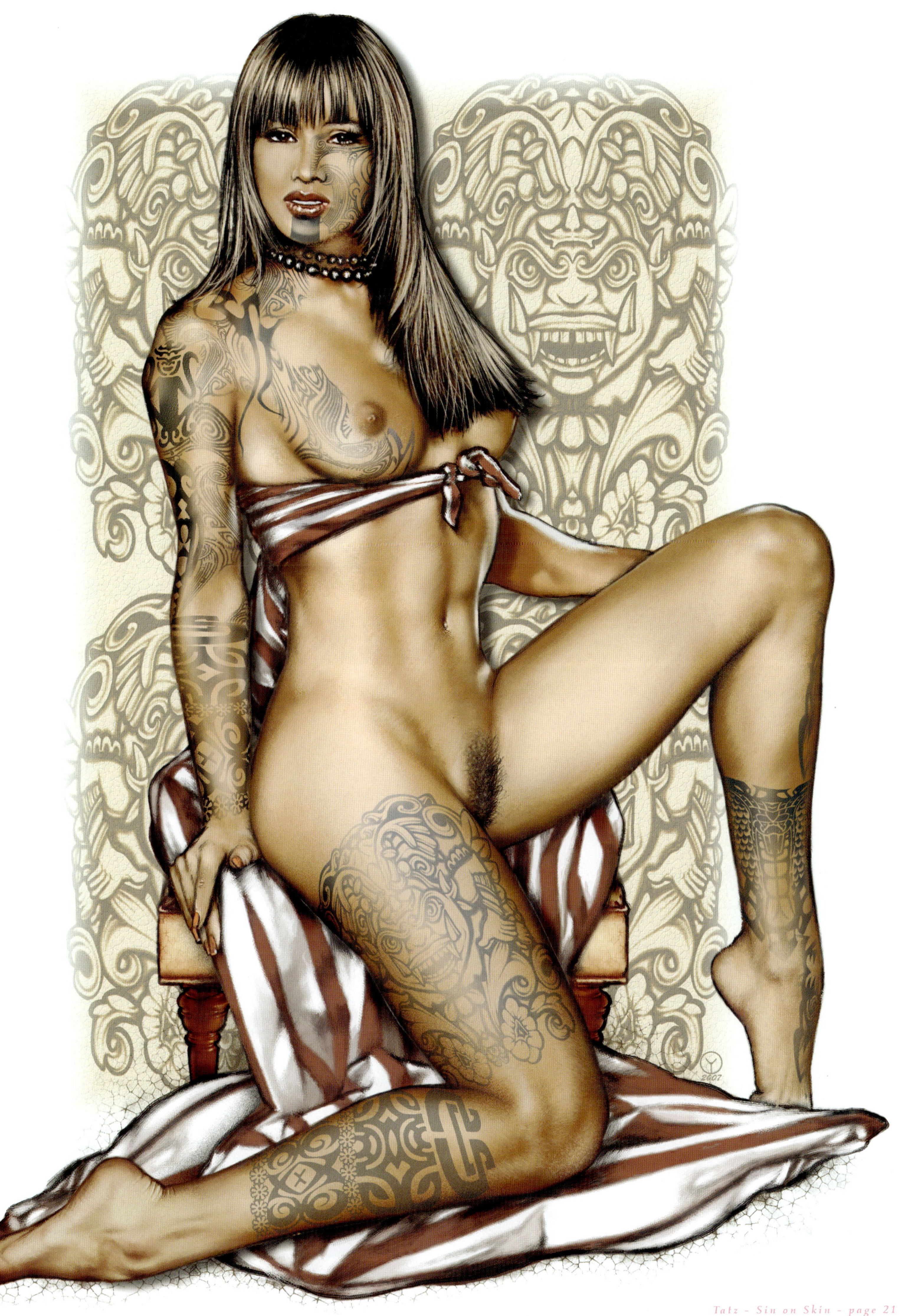

PONEKE CLAUDINE SHIPLEY

When I was 12 my father brought me to a rugby game; I went suddenly in love with that sport, but they were only males – so I was a little sad. When I was 17, I found a team with a coach who allowed me to train with them. When they saw the way I played, he sorted out the legal papers so I was able to play my rugby and I was happy. You can't imagine how many handsome boys were surprised when they held my breast to put me down.

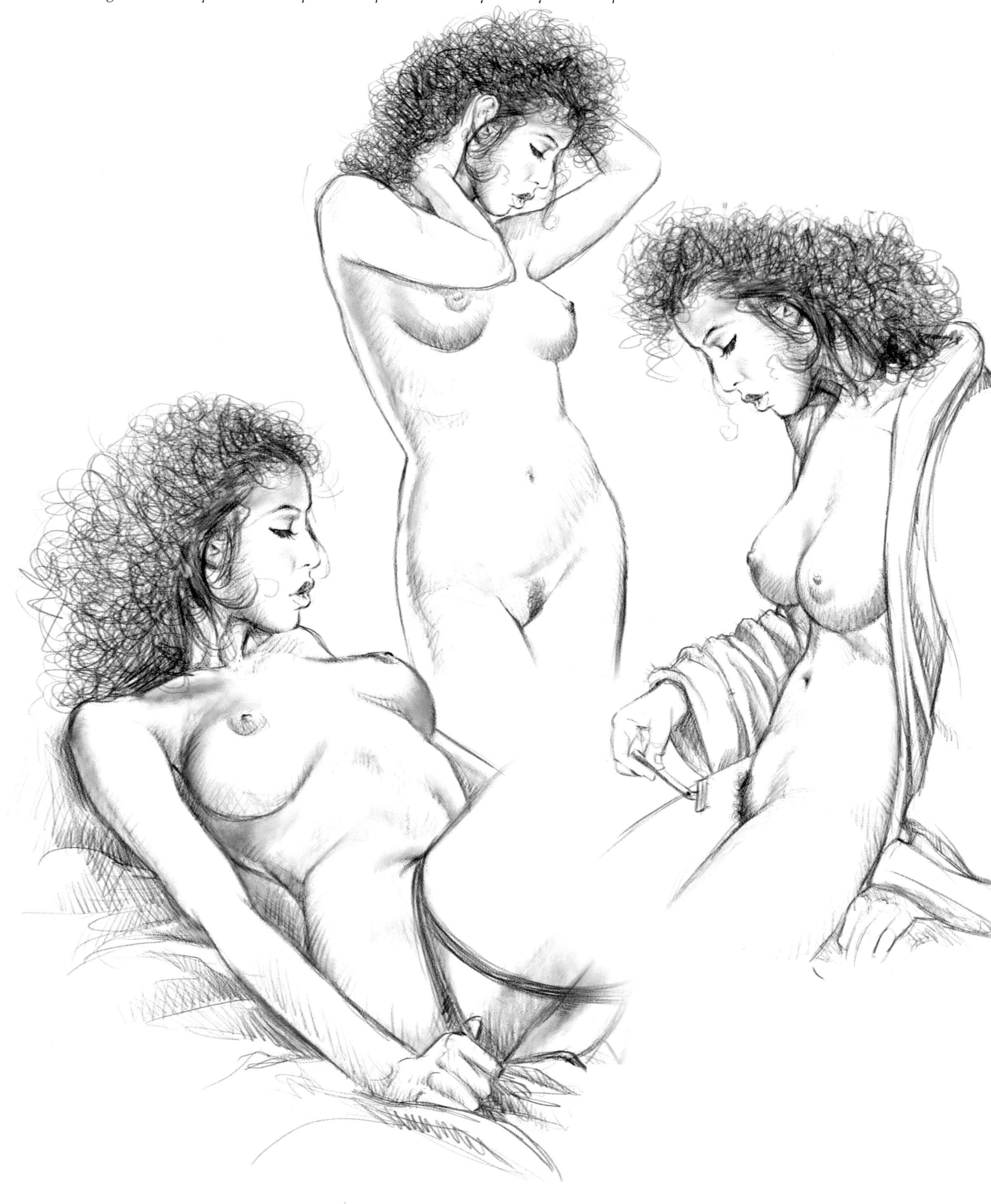

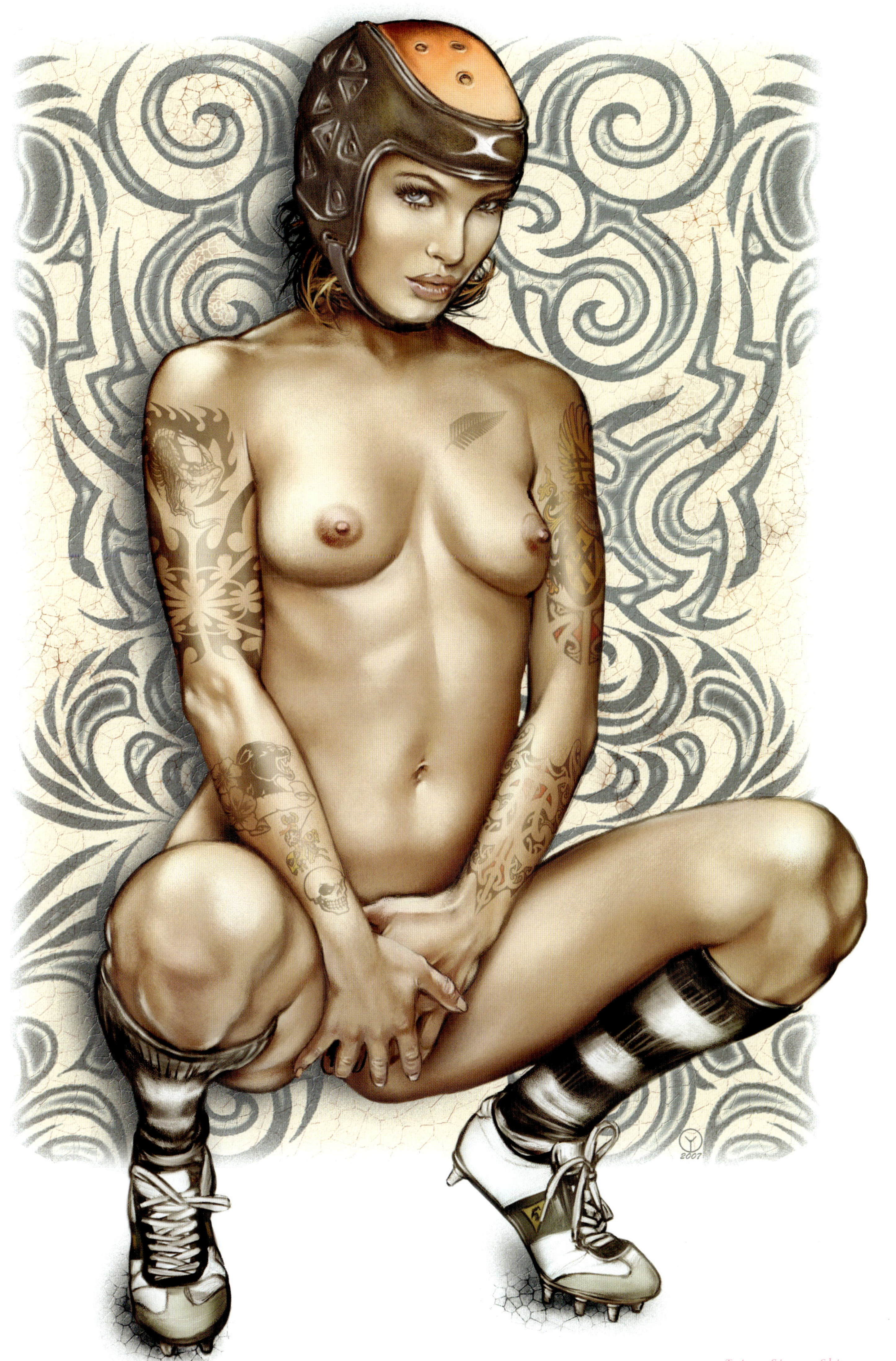

CAMMIE KIRKLAND

I'm a Texas girl from just outside of Austin. A fella asks me if I know my way around a rodeo, I just look at him and smile. "Who do you think invented the reverse Cowgirl with the surprise dismount?" Oh, they love it when I talk dirty!

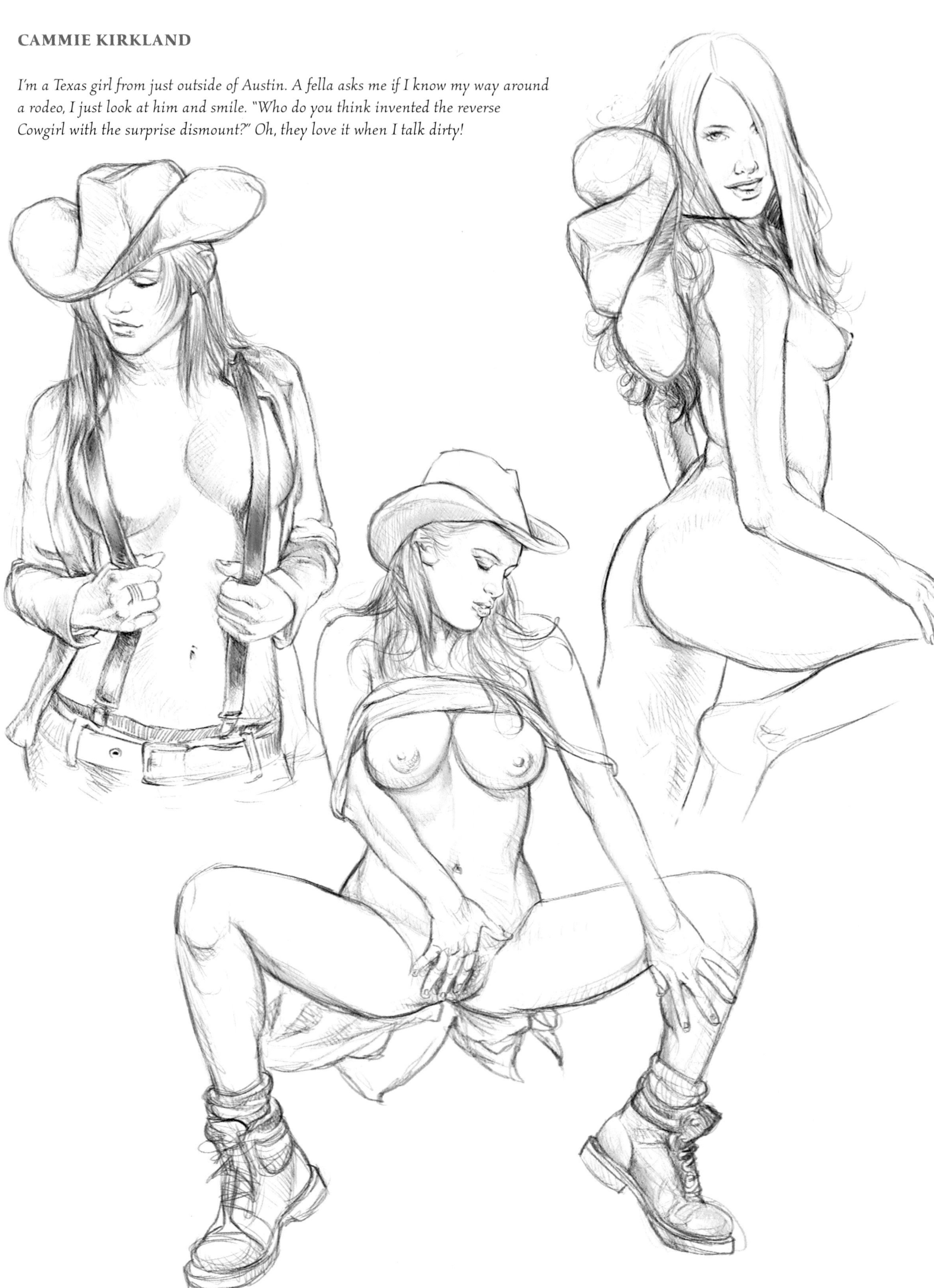

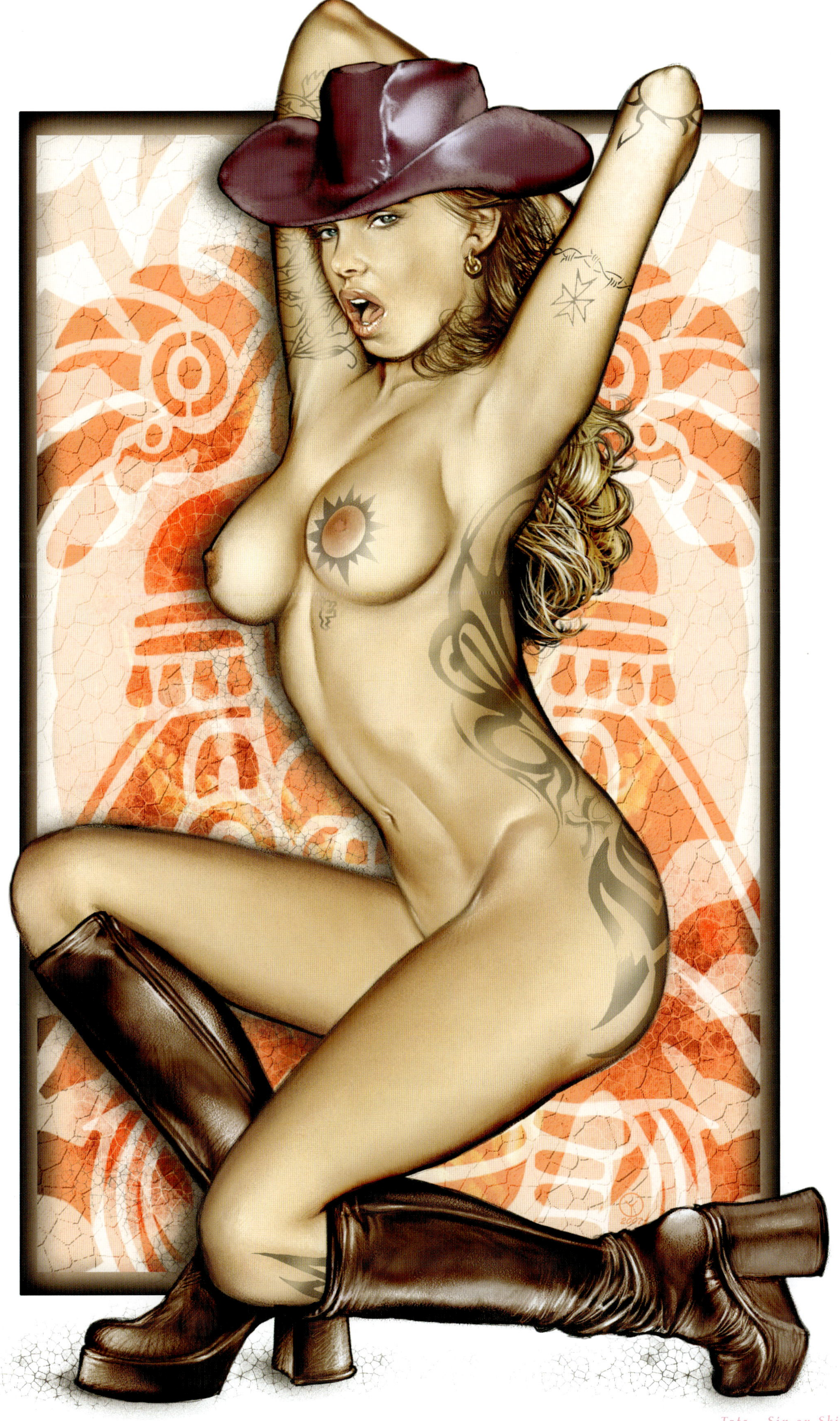

GEENA SANTACRUZ

My name is Geena Santacruz and I long to be part of a tribe!
Modern life has it's advantages, sure. Highspeed internet and coffee shops on every corner, that's great, but it's a little too civilized for my tastes. That's way I dig the tribal tattoo! It's timeless – it's ancient and connects us to the past.
It says to people, don't get too comfortable. Don't forget – all this modern shit could be stripped away in a second, and we could all be foraging for food in the forests. It also reminds us we're all human, and all part of the same tribe!

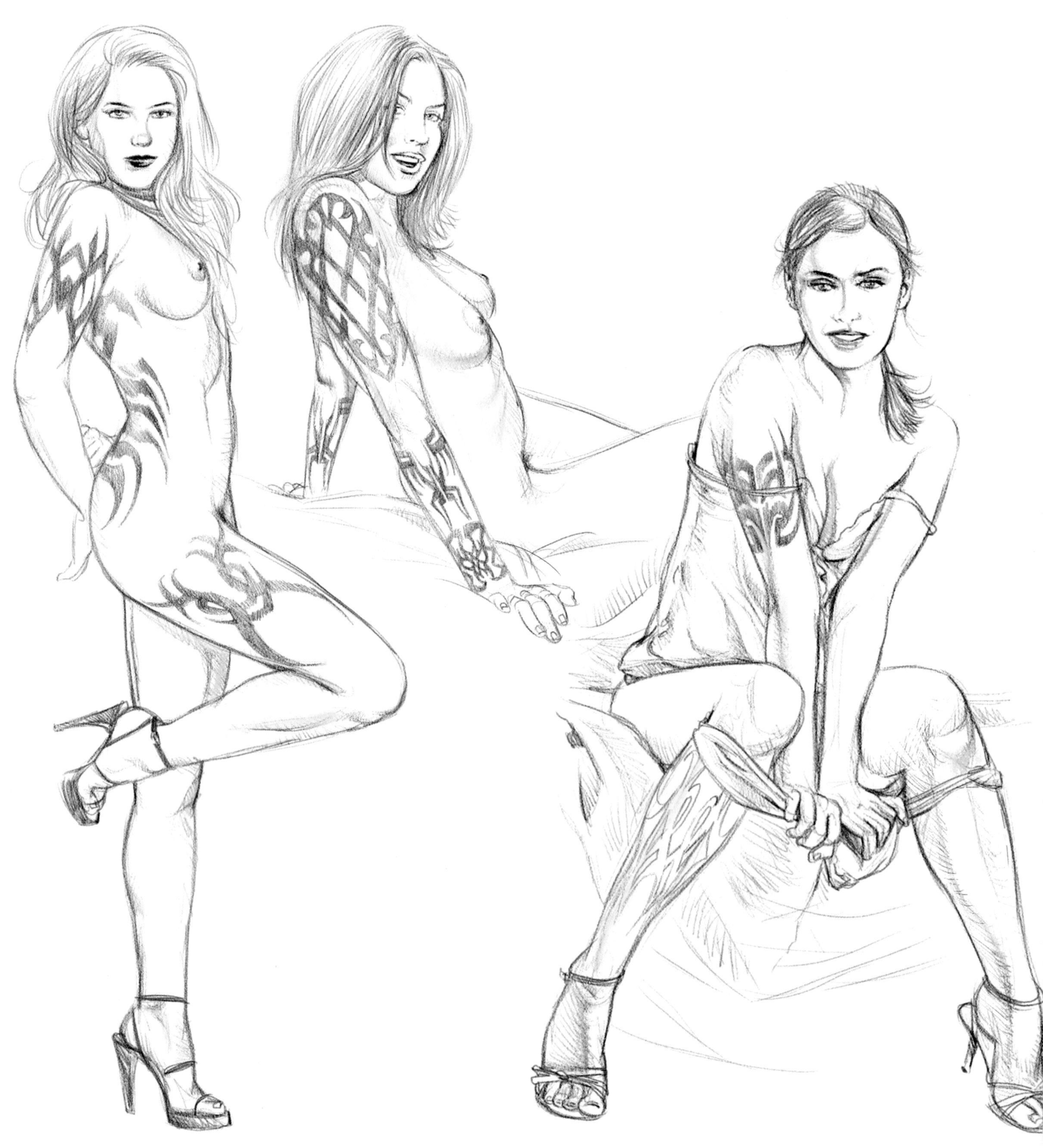

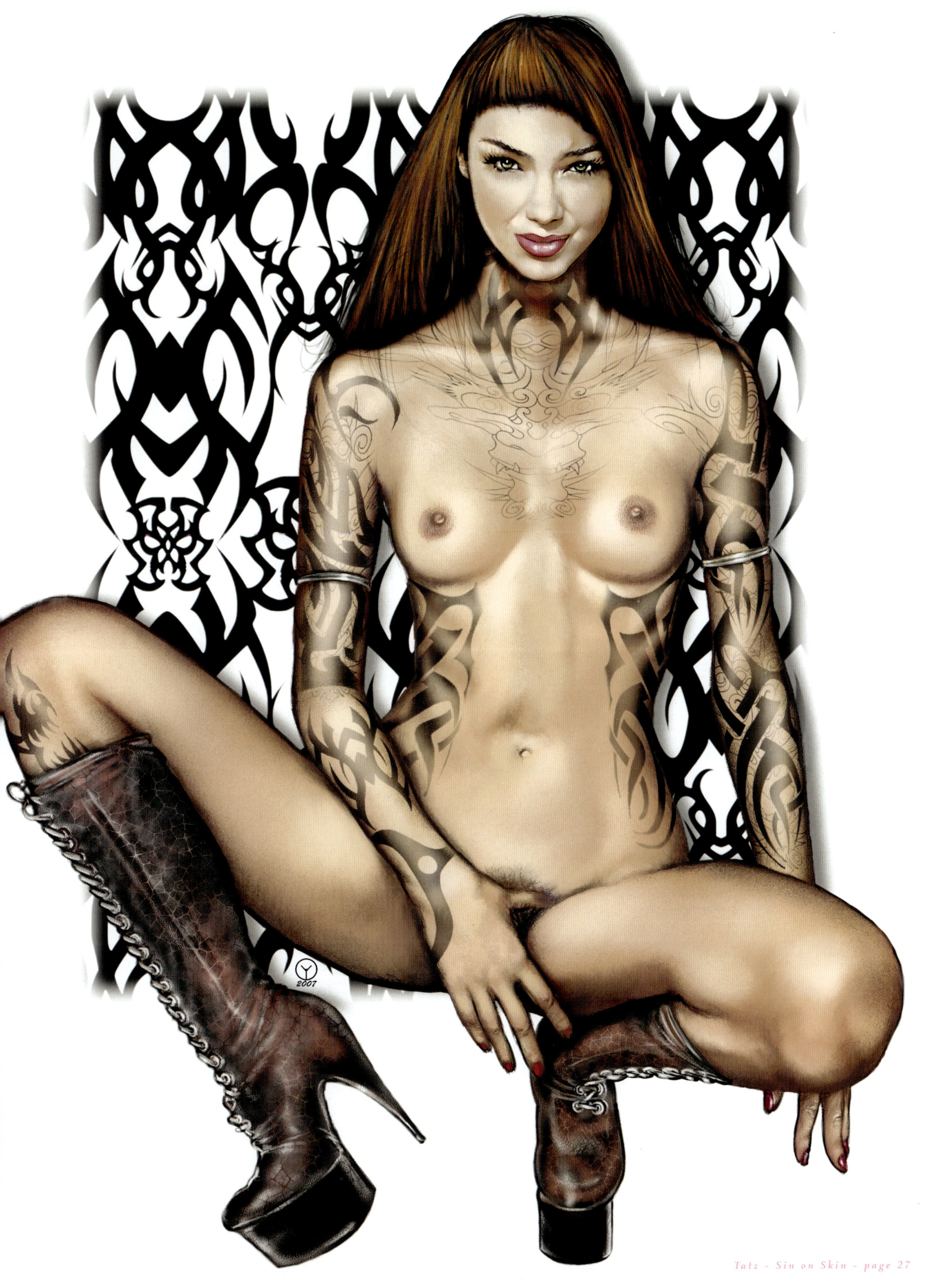
2007

JOANNE McIVERNESS

Clearly I'm not some flame-haired Celtic Queen, ready to do battle with the Roman Empire (but I often wish I was!)
My mother was a bit of an ass-kicker, born in Bolivia. My father was French, very sweet but not very macho (okay, according to my Mom, borderline gay). I think I was blessed with their best qualities. I know when to fight, and when to fuck!.
My husband is from Holland, and plays drums in a tribal Hungarian band.
He has a little dick and a great love for me, that's why I married him. I am the only wife or girlfriend that goes on tour with the band.
I'm the best kind of groupie to have – the one that keeps the filthy little bitches away, and just lets the really cute ones backstage!
I've even been known to sample a few myself.
Guess Daddy's not the only borderline gay in the family!

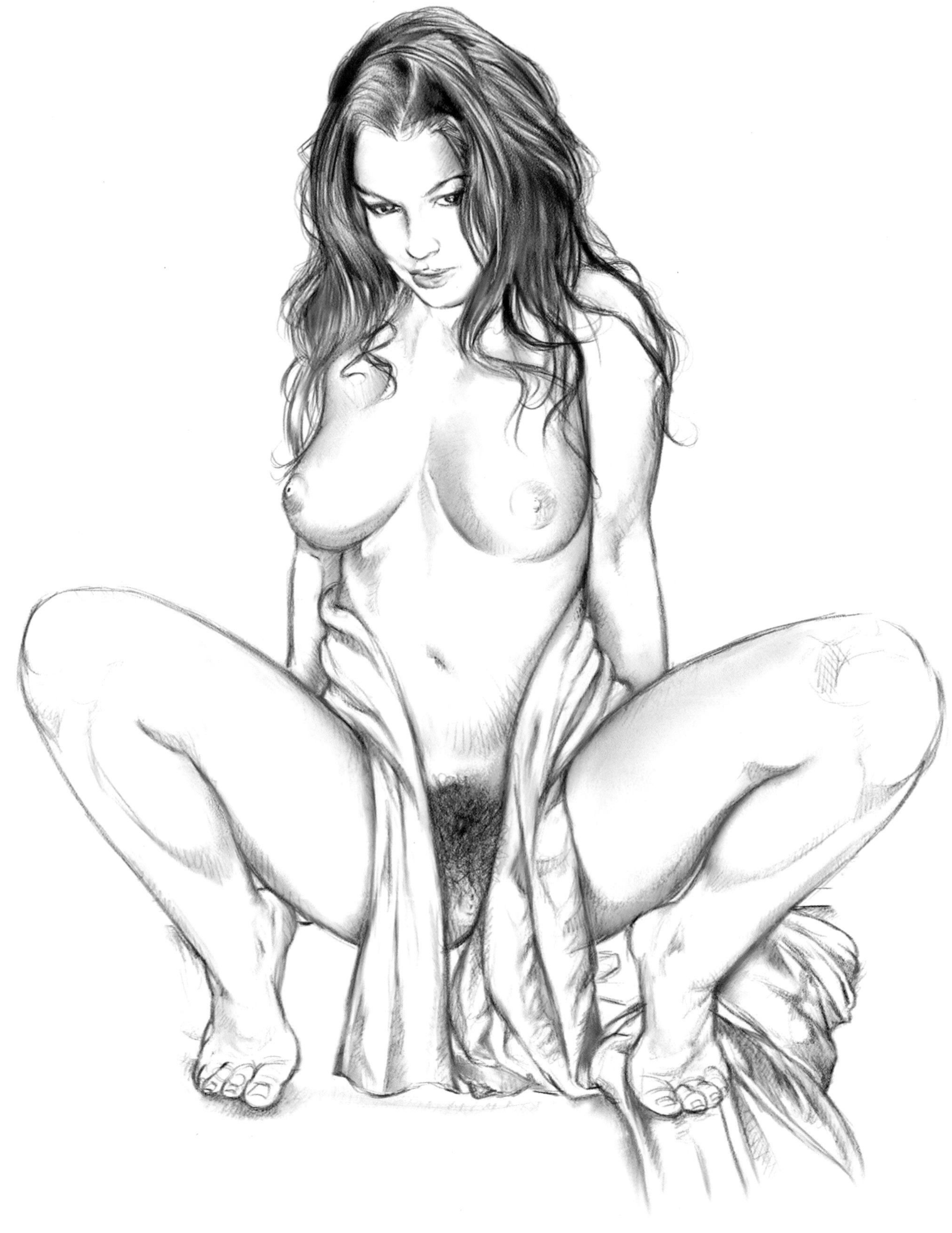

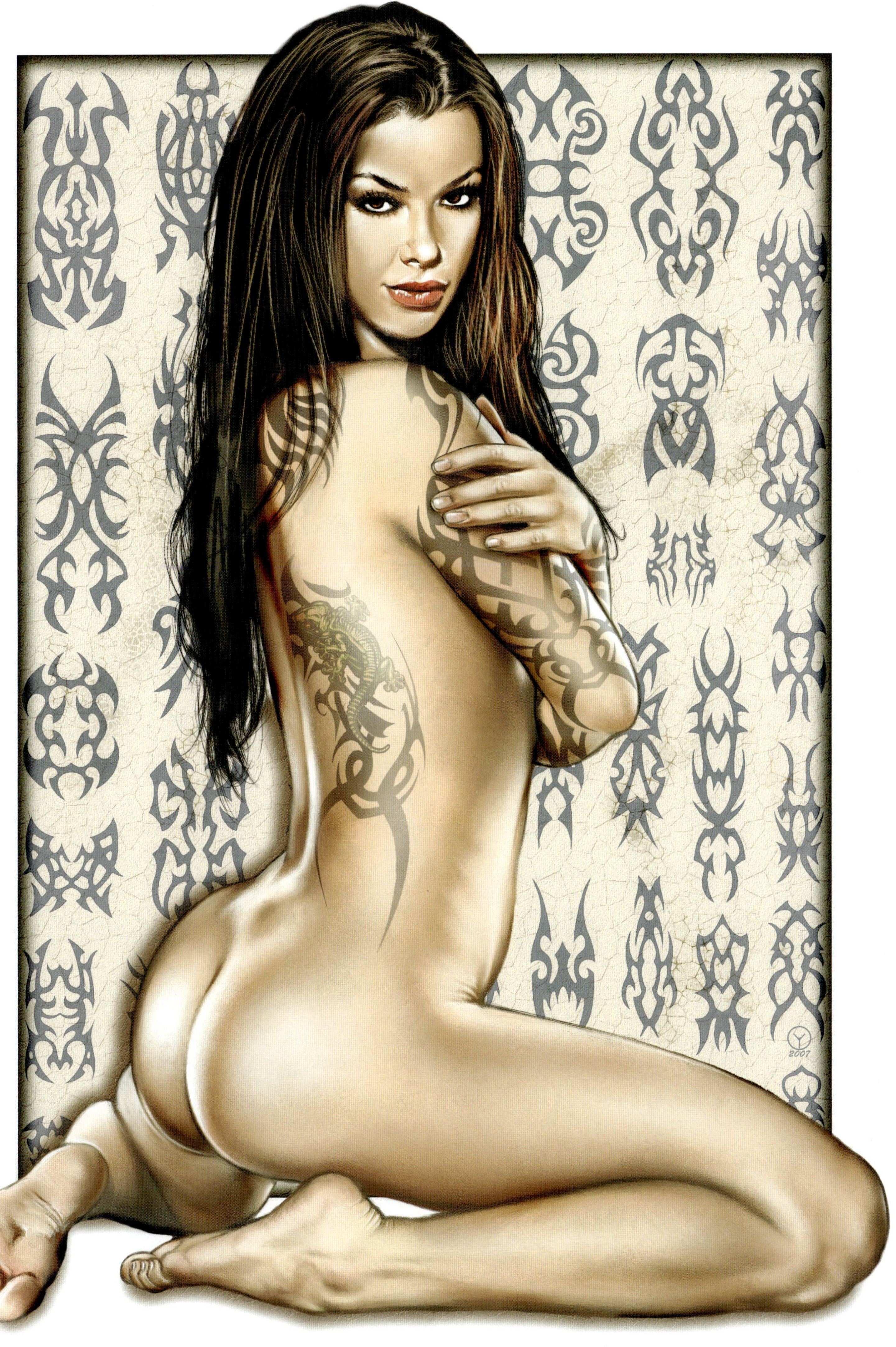

TIGER BEAST

Tigers have massive sharp teeth in their mouths to defend themselves and to find food in the jungle.
Me, I haven't got massive sharp teeth in my mouth. So where am I hiding them?
Are you so brave to put one of your fingers .. do have I to tell you where?
I'm joking, of course...

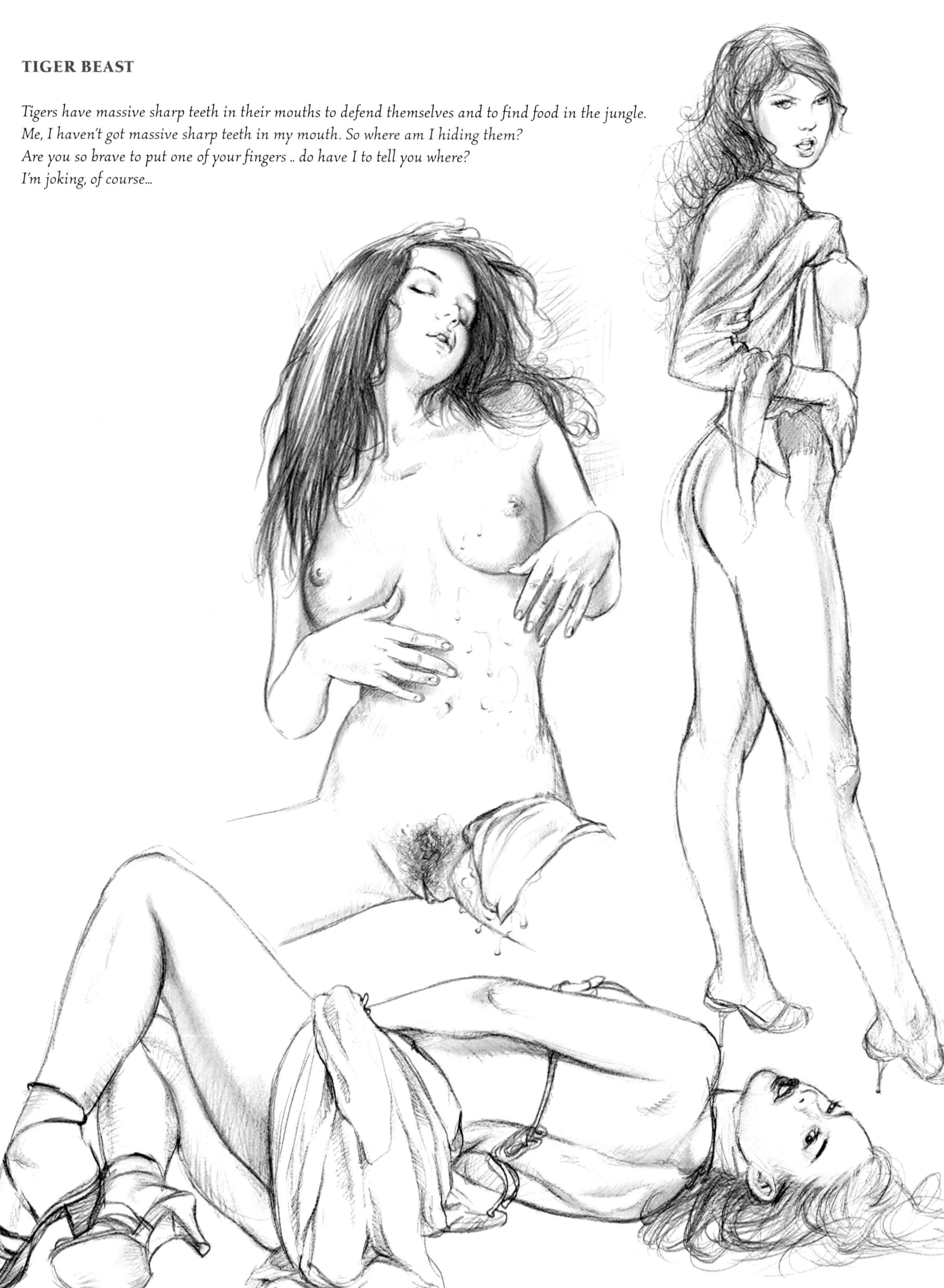

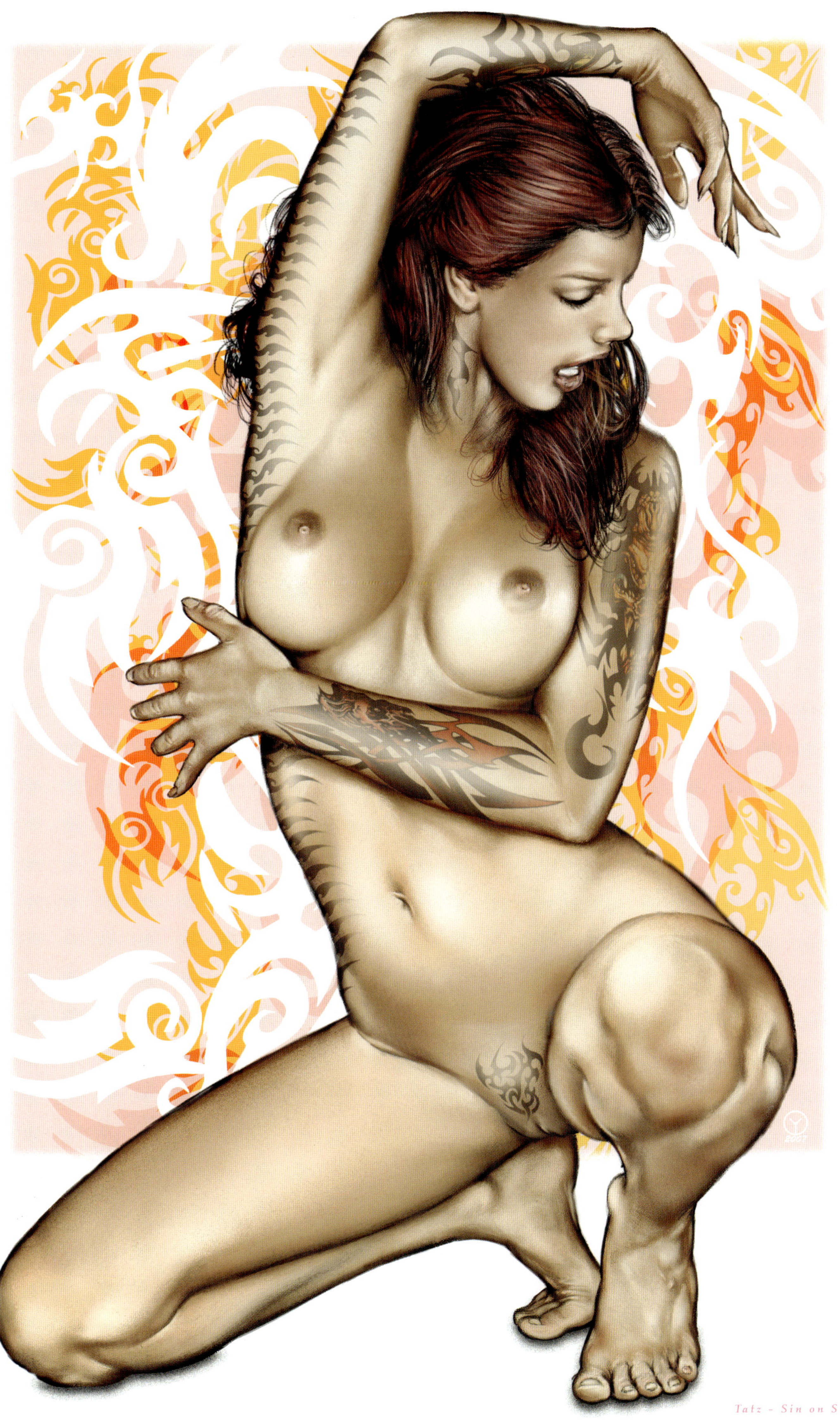

IVETTE

Ivette from Angouleme was going to Bordeaux. Ivette from Angouleme stole a couple of boots in Grenoble.
Ivette from Angouleme has a skull and a cross on her right arm and a perfumed flower on the other one.
Both arms were tattooed by Sebastien from Lille.
Ivette from Angouleme bought some butter in Paris.
Ivette from Angouleme had a yellow beret that Victor, a friend from Nantes, gave her as a present.
Ivette from Angouleme colored her hair red in Strasbourg.
Ivette from Angouleme has left her heart and her soul in Aiaccio.

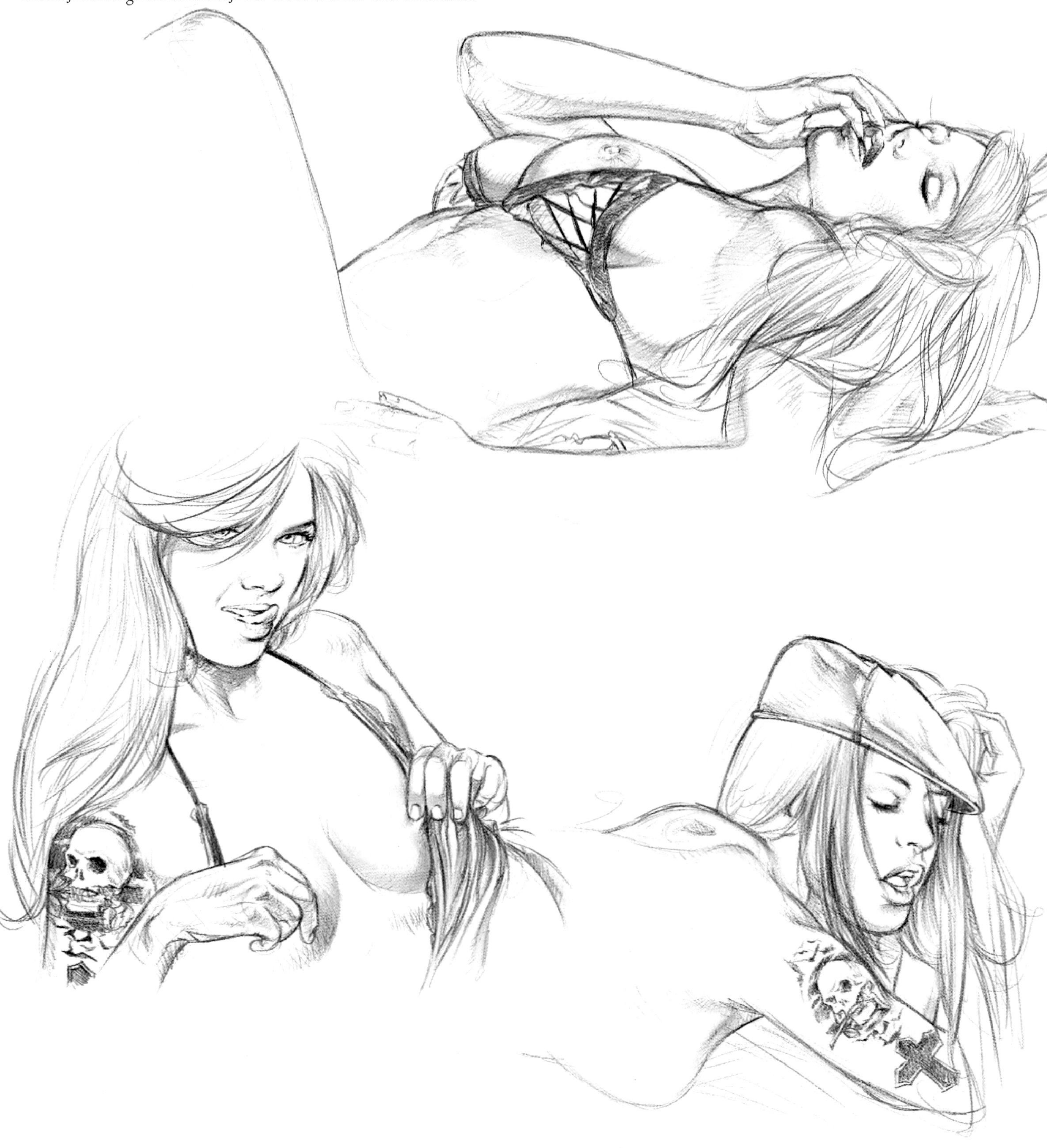

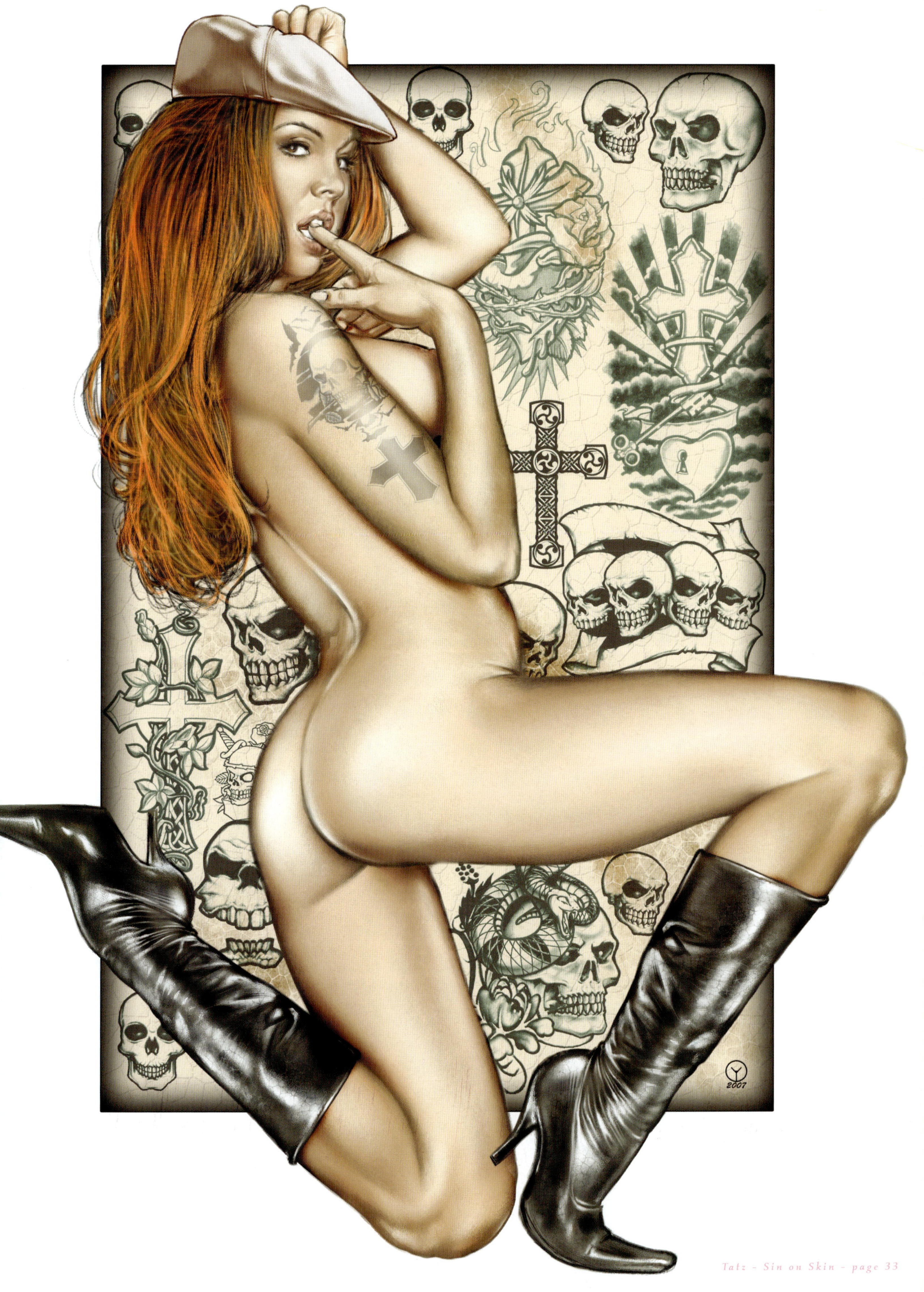

SELINA KILE

My name is Selina Kile. I chose it when I was twelve.
I also let my skin have its first tattoo at that time. It was a cat. I did it myself with a ballpoint pen.
When my parents saw it, they freaked. I didn't care. It was fierce!
When I got older, I got more permanent cats attached to my skin. First in areas only I knew about, then eventually, ones the whole world could enjoy. And pet. If they asked nicely!
Want to pet my pussy? Let me get these panties off!

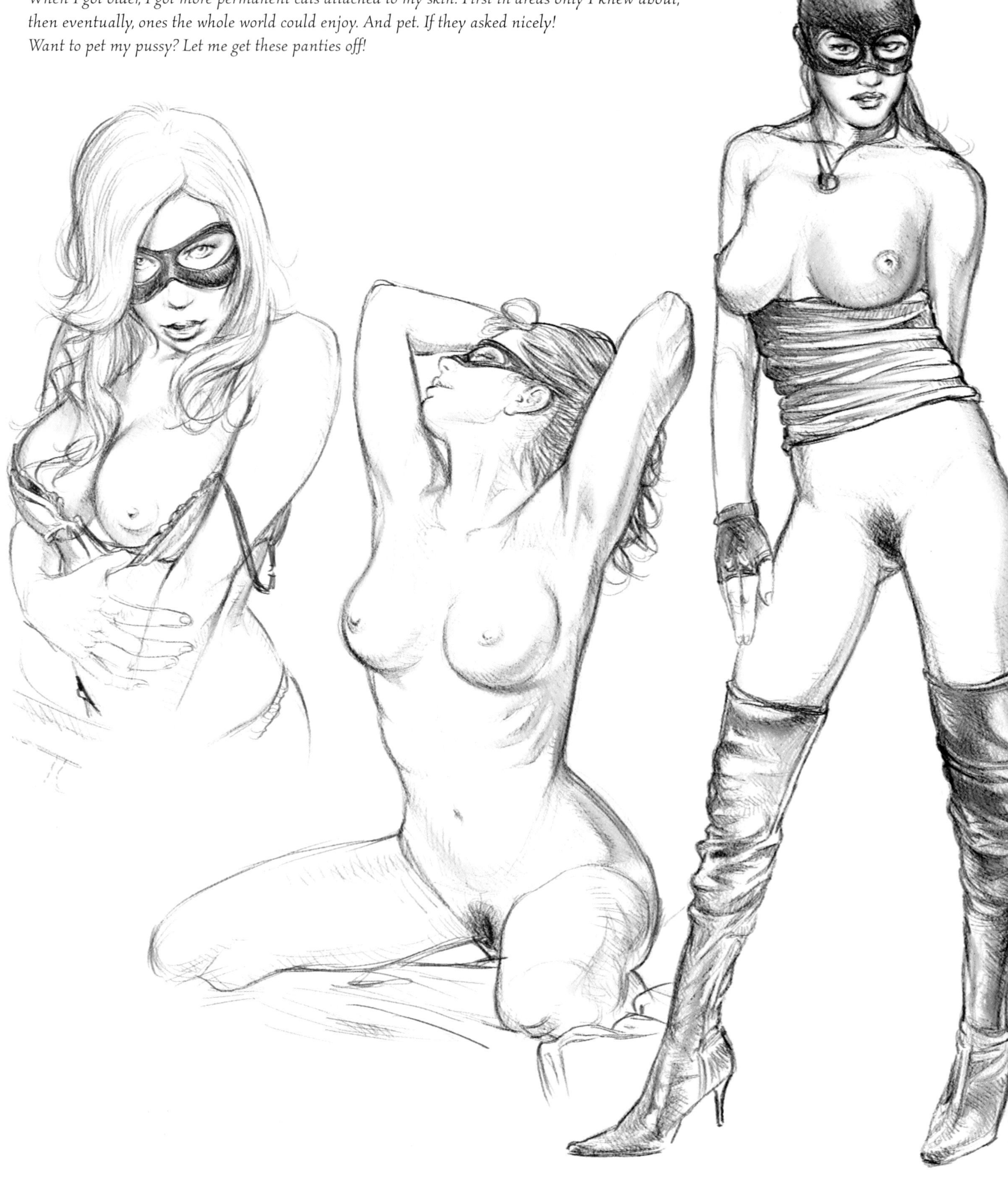

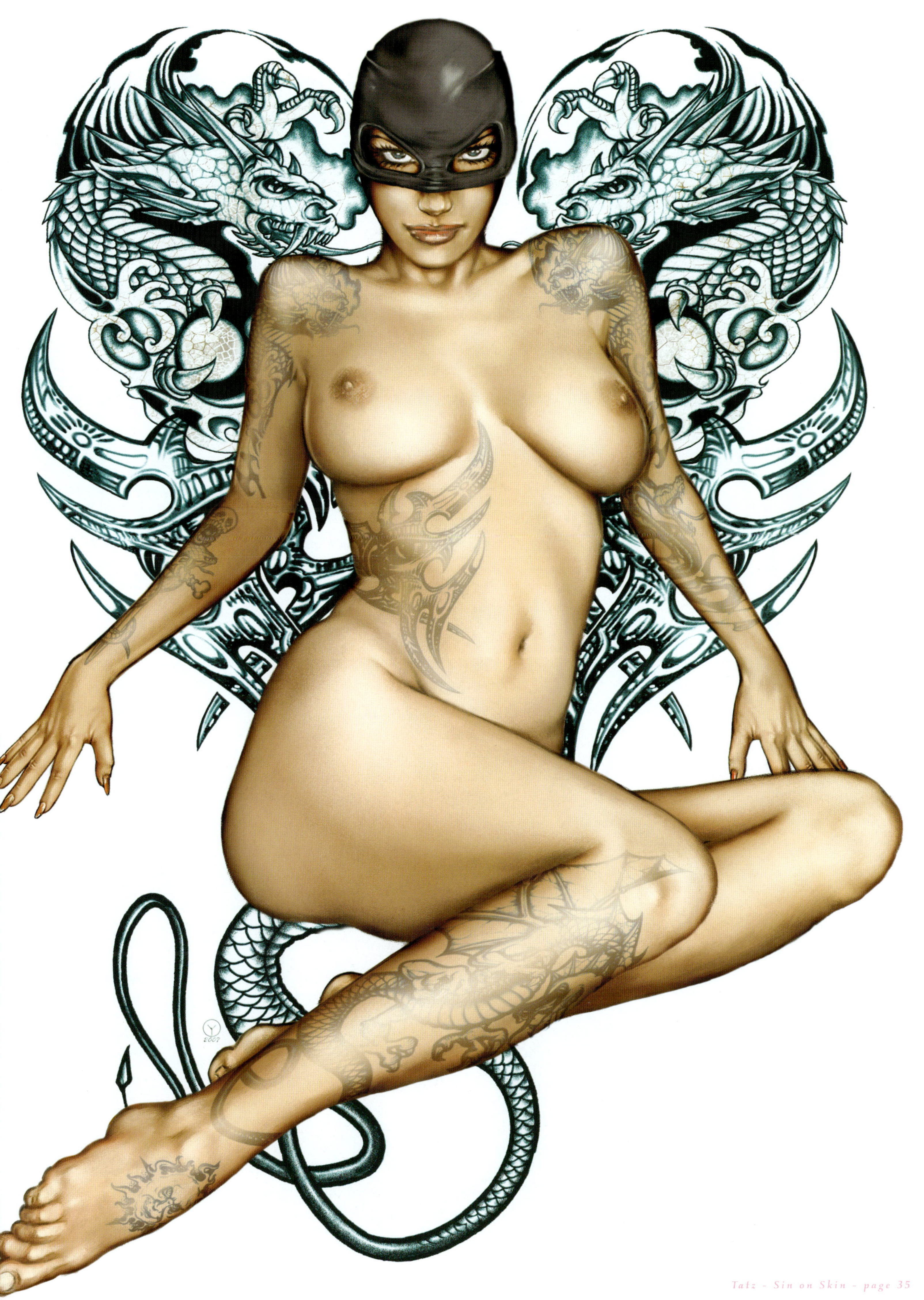

SARA VALLICELLI

Ever since I was a little kid, people have been trying to get me to conform. Mom, Dad, Gammy, my brother Dave, and even my gay brother Mark! Jeezus! If he doesn't get "Standing out from a crowd", who would?! I was always the chick who'd flash her tits at the home game, or wear a short skirt without panties. Hey, joke 'em if they can't take a fuck, right? So, when my friend Didi got her first tattoo, I was SO there! But I wasn't about to get some little girly-girl heart on my left ass-cheek! I say go for broke, baby! I'm just gettin' started! See me when I'm 20 – I'll be head to toe tatted!

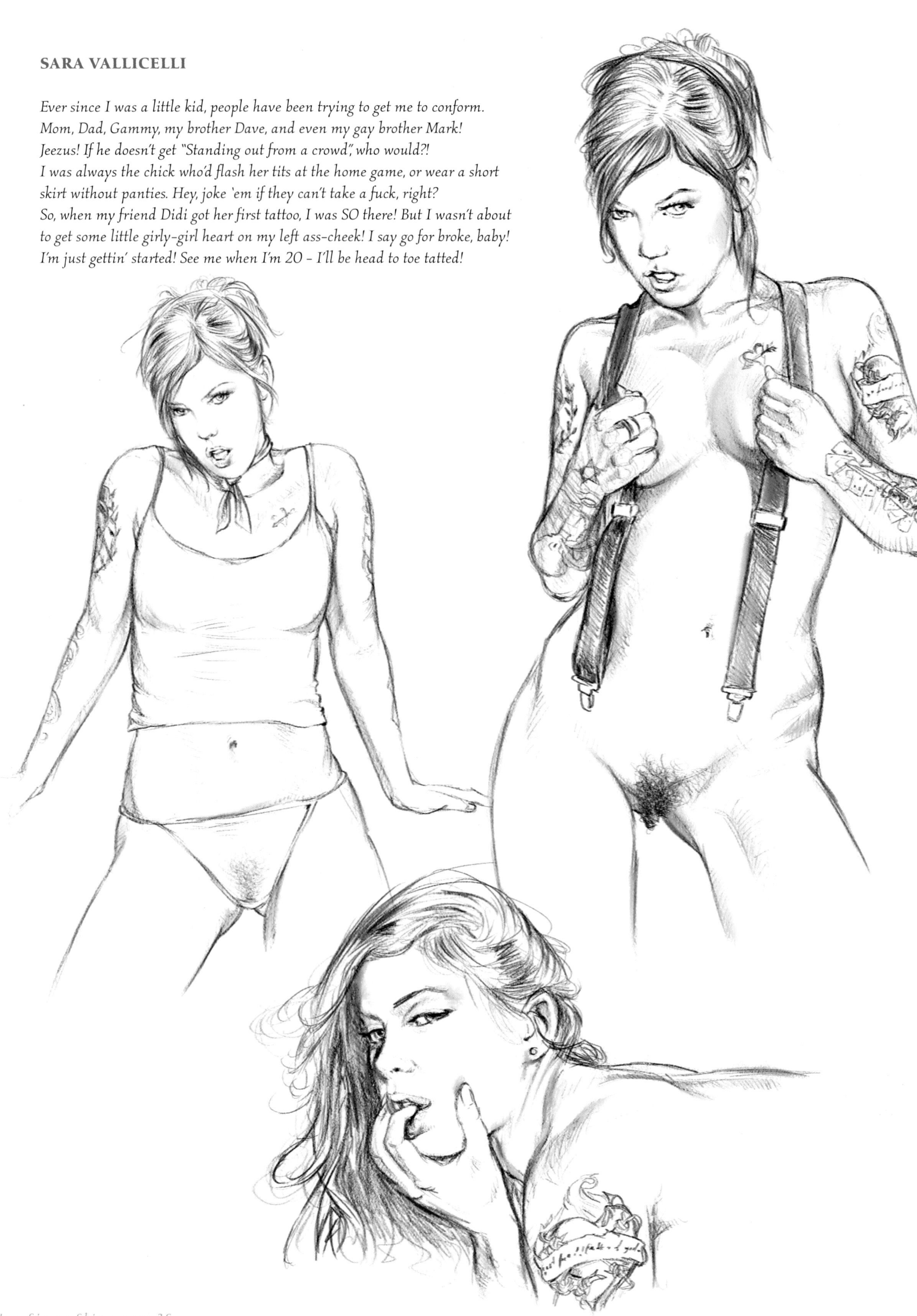

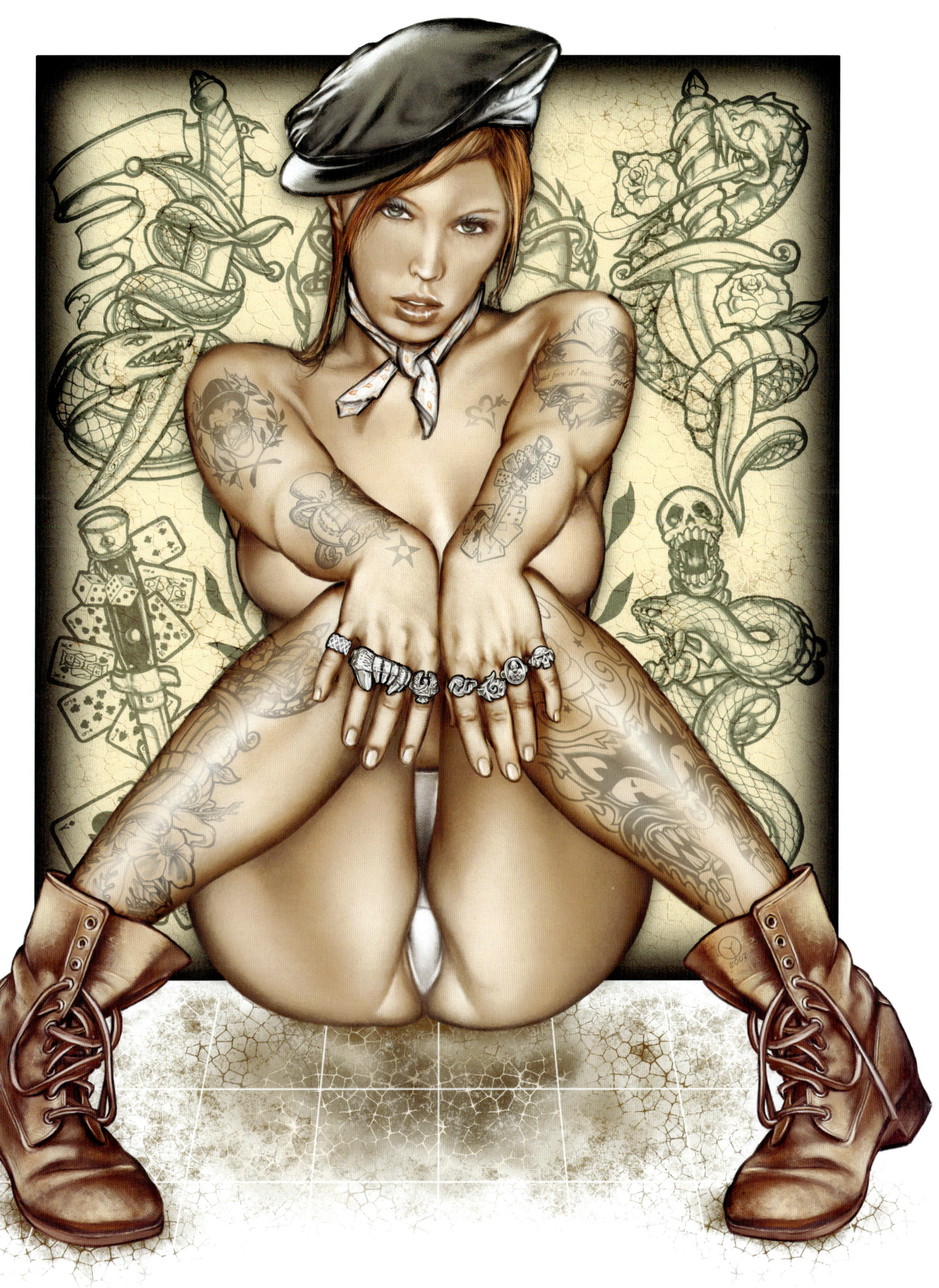

GIULIANA DALLA BOTTE

Although my surname is of aristocratic origin, I'm a whore and everybody knows me as "Giuliana La Puttana", an Italian way to say what I am.
But what is a whore, but someone who does something for money, eh?
Tonight I have a first class client in my alcove, he is a general manager from Cheney; every time he is back in my town he calls me to meet me during the night. Six months ago he told me he's got a fetish for tattoos, and he'd pay me triple my fee if I could accommodate him I told him I couldn't do anything like that to myself permanently (I DO have other clients!), but I'd be happy to see if I could come up with a compromise.
Then I thought...Henna! And there's a lovely Indian woman who works at a local restaurant who'd be happy to do it for me - a very small fee.
So, the general manager, he's happy.
The henna artist, she's happy.
And me, I'm getting triple my usual money. So sure - I'm happy too!

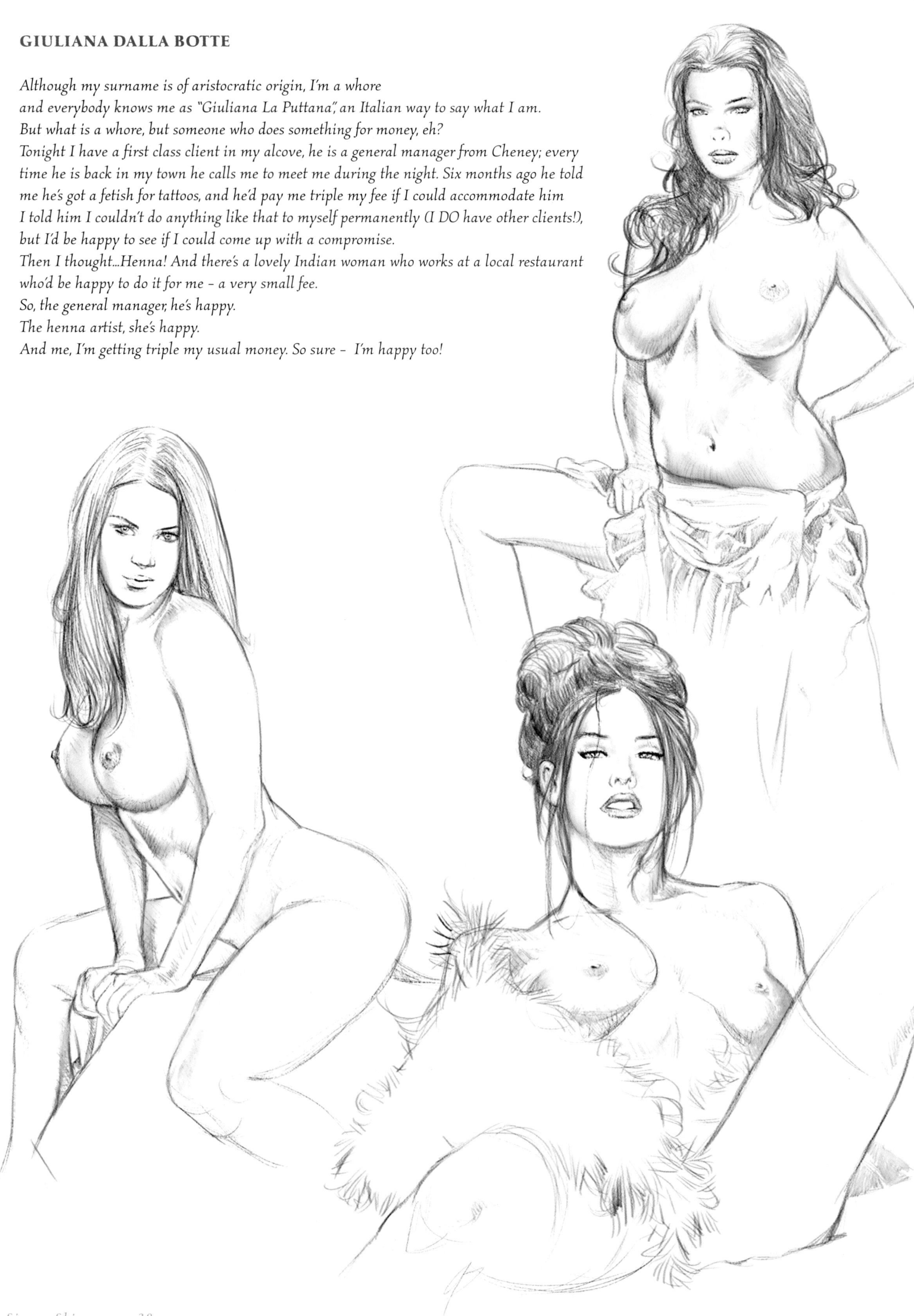

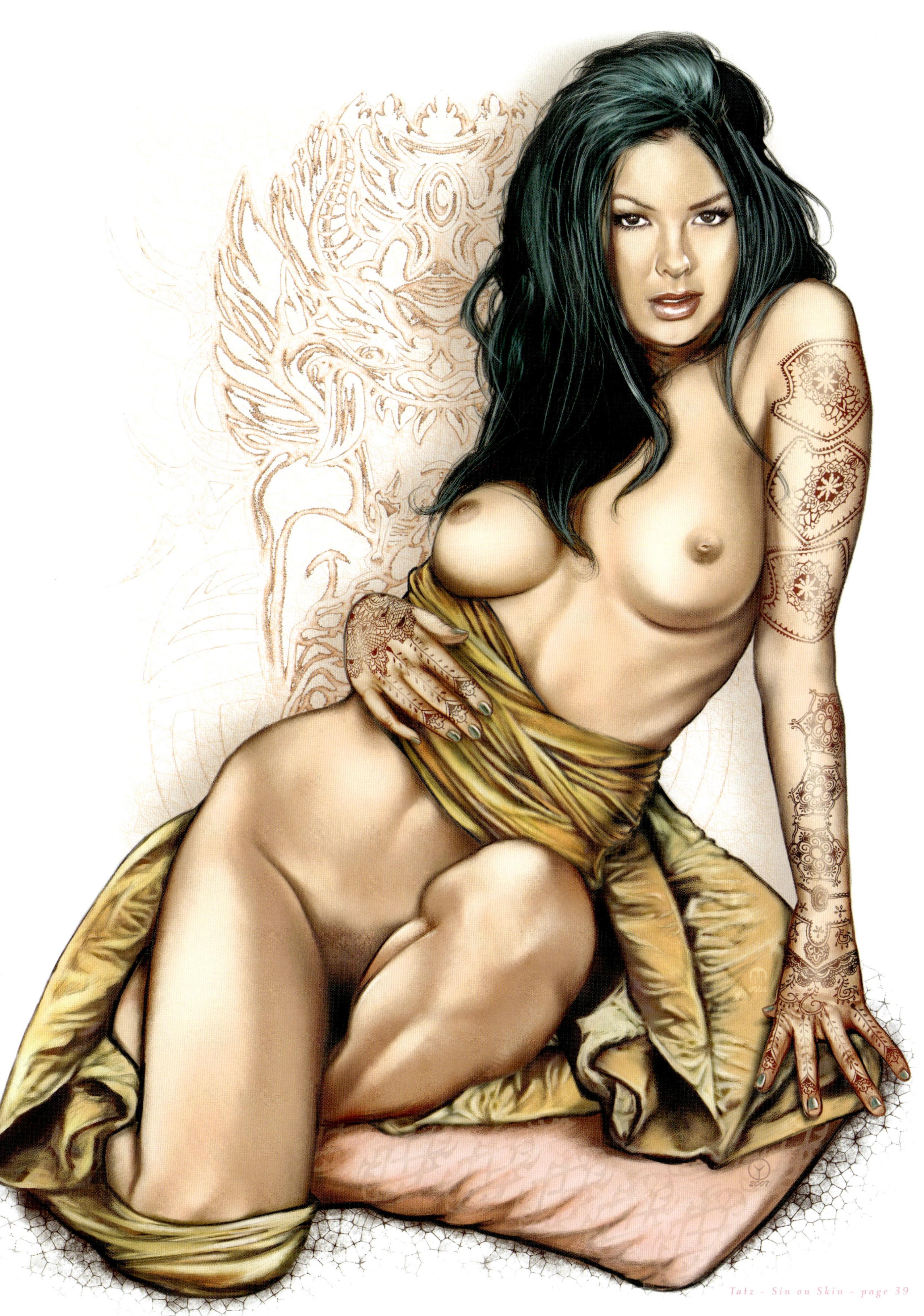

MARICA BACESCU

Yes, I have growned up in Sighisoara, Romania.
I am there to have a little of the lot that many have there.
I hoped thut you lefd me live there to be like you be. I always liked a lot what you are.
And I want to be with you. No, excuse me, like you. Have you see my hands?

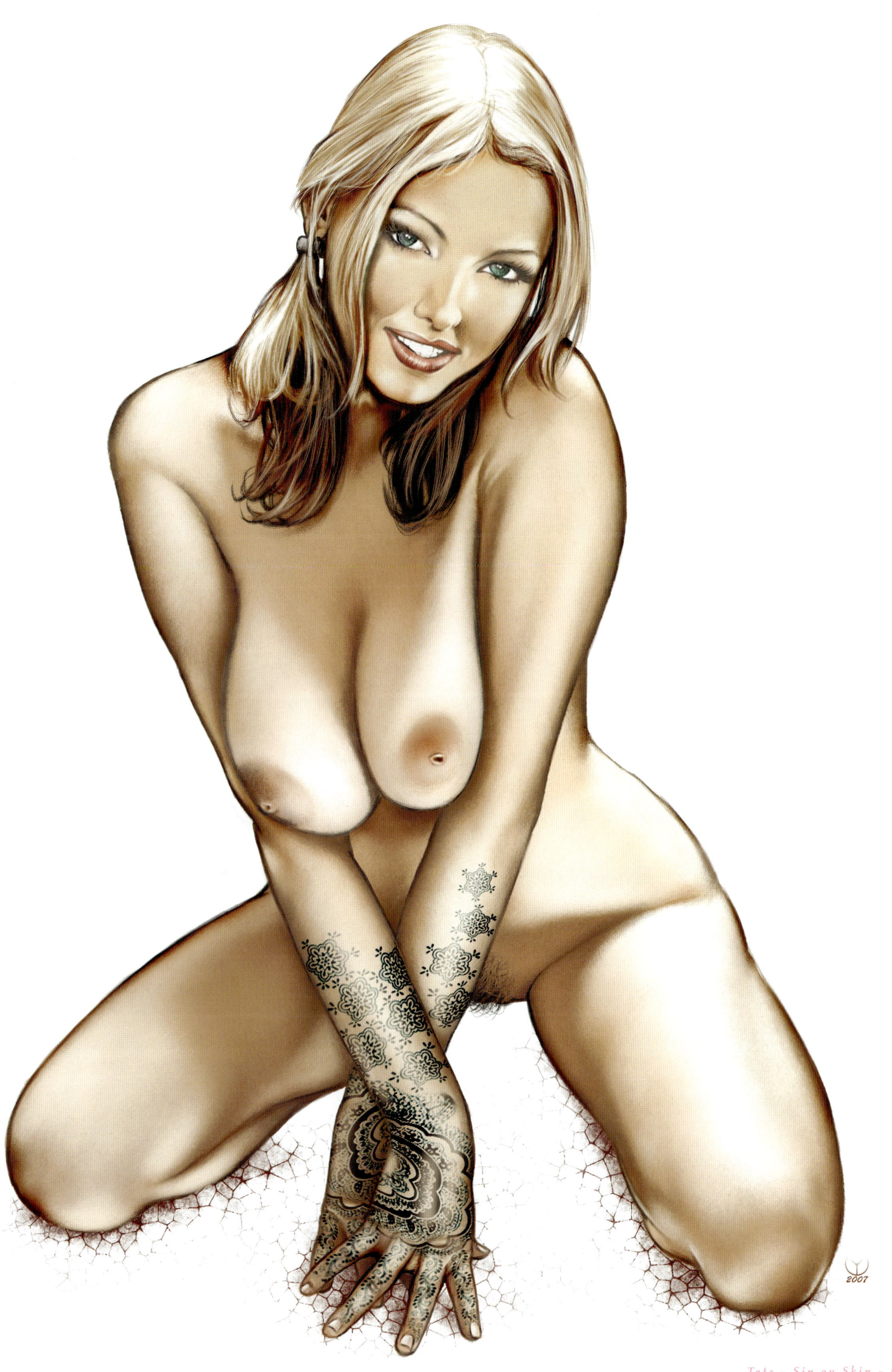
2007

MICAELA USTERDUCTCH

Tonight they will remember me as a star. They will award a prize to me as the first actress who was able to change her life from XXX-movies to Bollywood films. Now I can be sexy without being naked and I have decided to dress in Armani. Next year they will award a similar prize to me to be able to come back to XXX-movies after having appreciated the cajolery of Bombay, because deep down in my soul, I am the same whore you've always known.

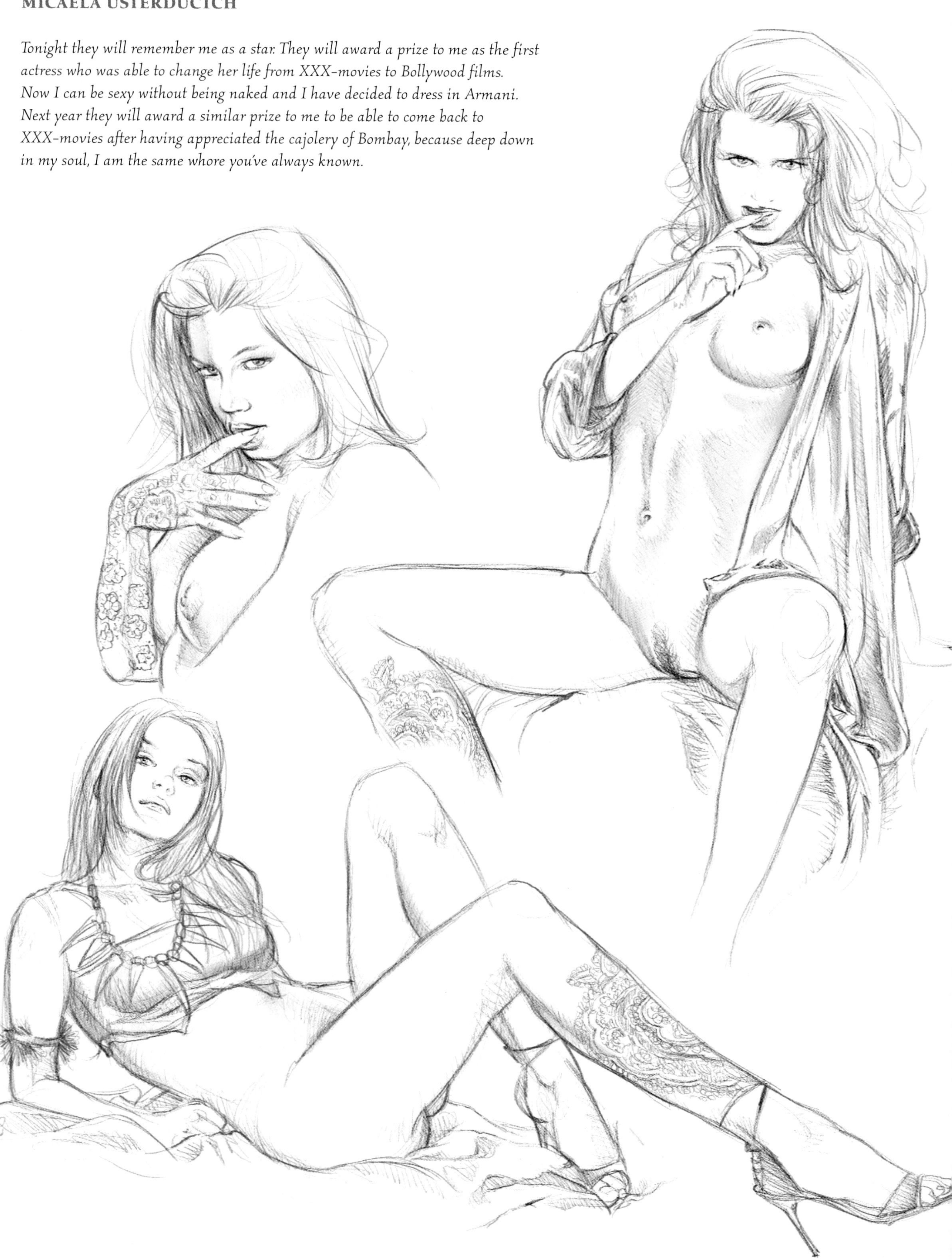

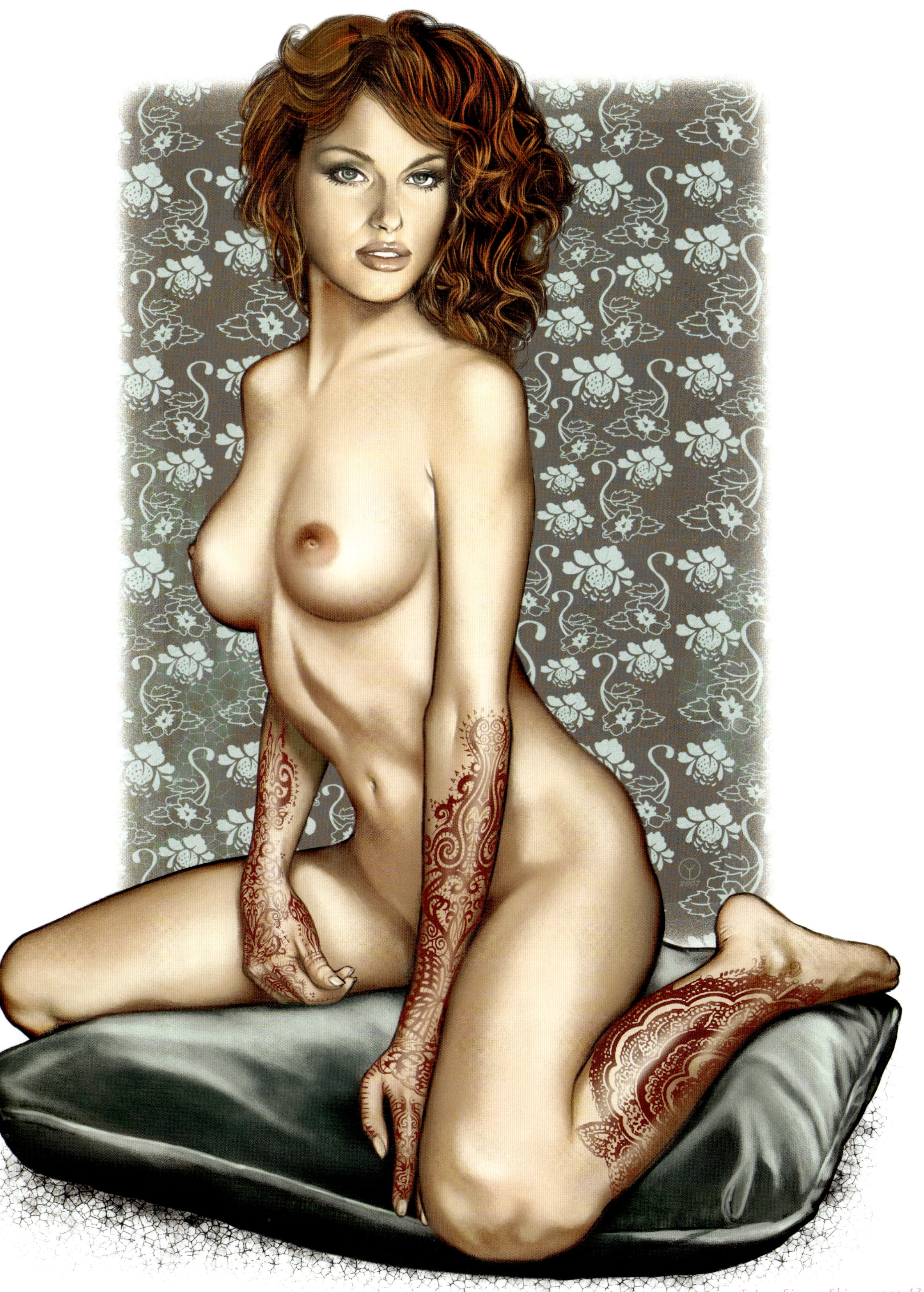

VALENTINA SUTTER

My name is Valentina. I love a lot dragons. I like the way they spit all their strength outside. The flames from the mouth. It is something I did when I'm in love and fuckin,' they say. You can't believe how many four-letter words I spit when I'm in bed making love. Making sex. I'm a photographer. I live in Milan. Ok, that's all.

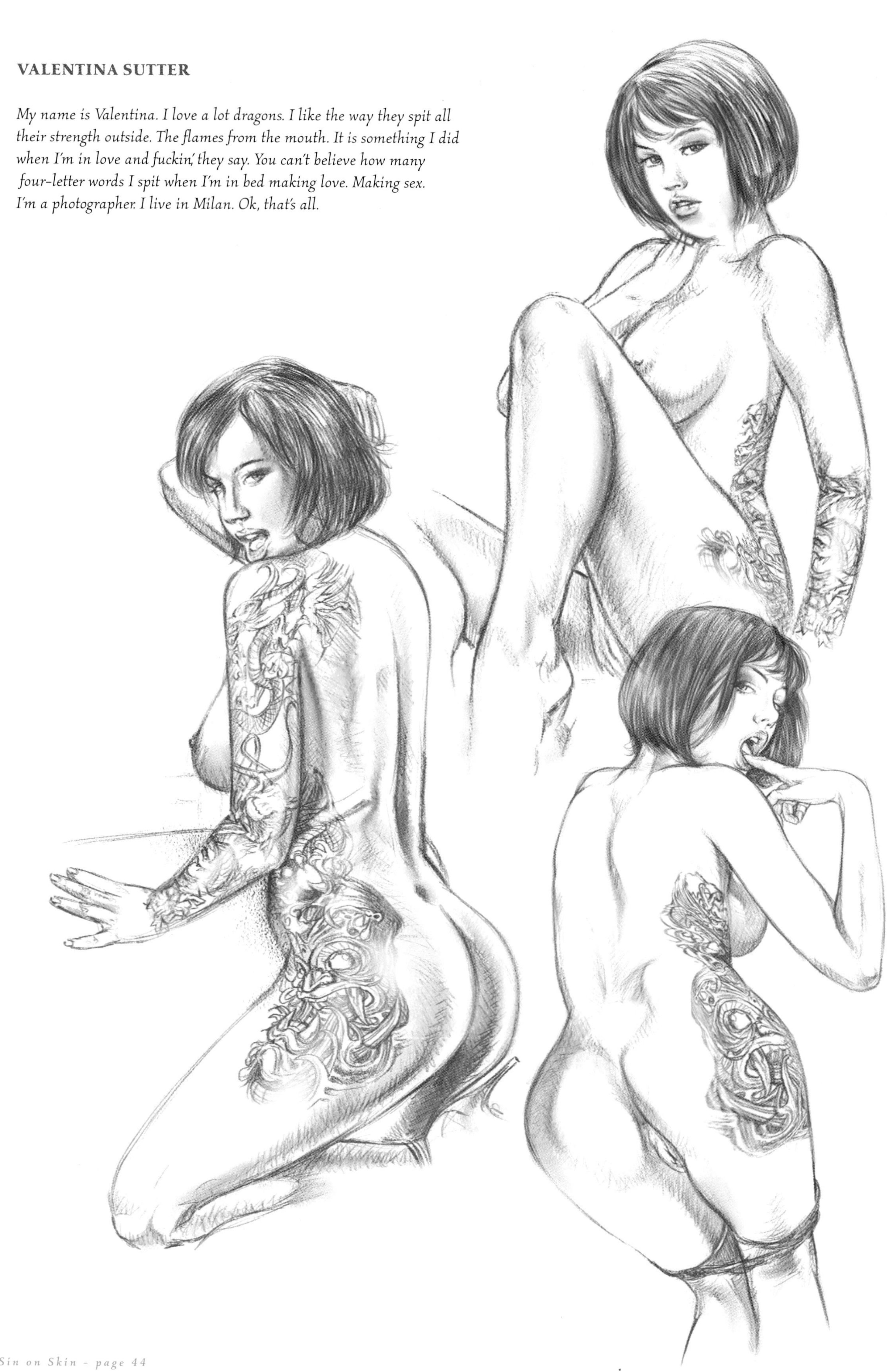

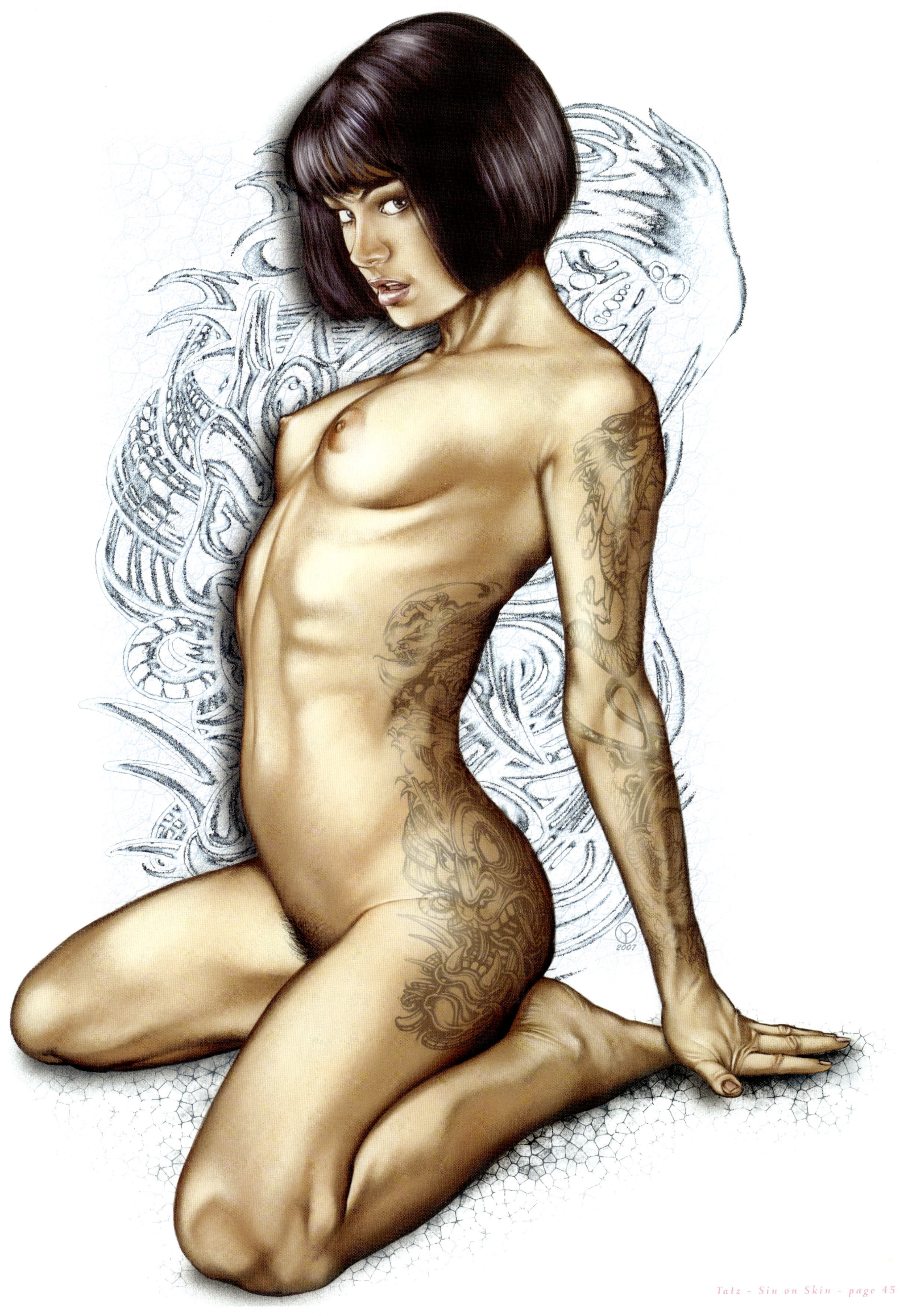
2007

CAMINSKY VAN DER SARR

Yes you can fuck my ass if you want.
Yes you can have your dick in my mouth, if you want.
If you want you can have your dick in my mouth after it's been in my ass.
I am able to make love with your wife, if you want and she wants.
You can come between my tits, if you prefer.
Only don't touch the skin of my back, because the tattoo is brand new.

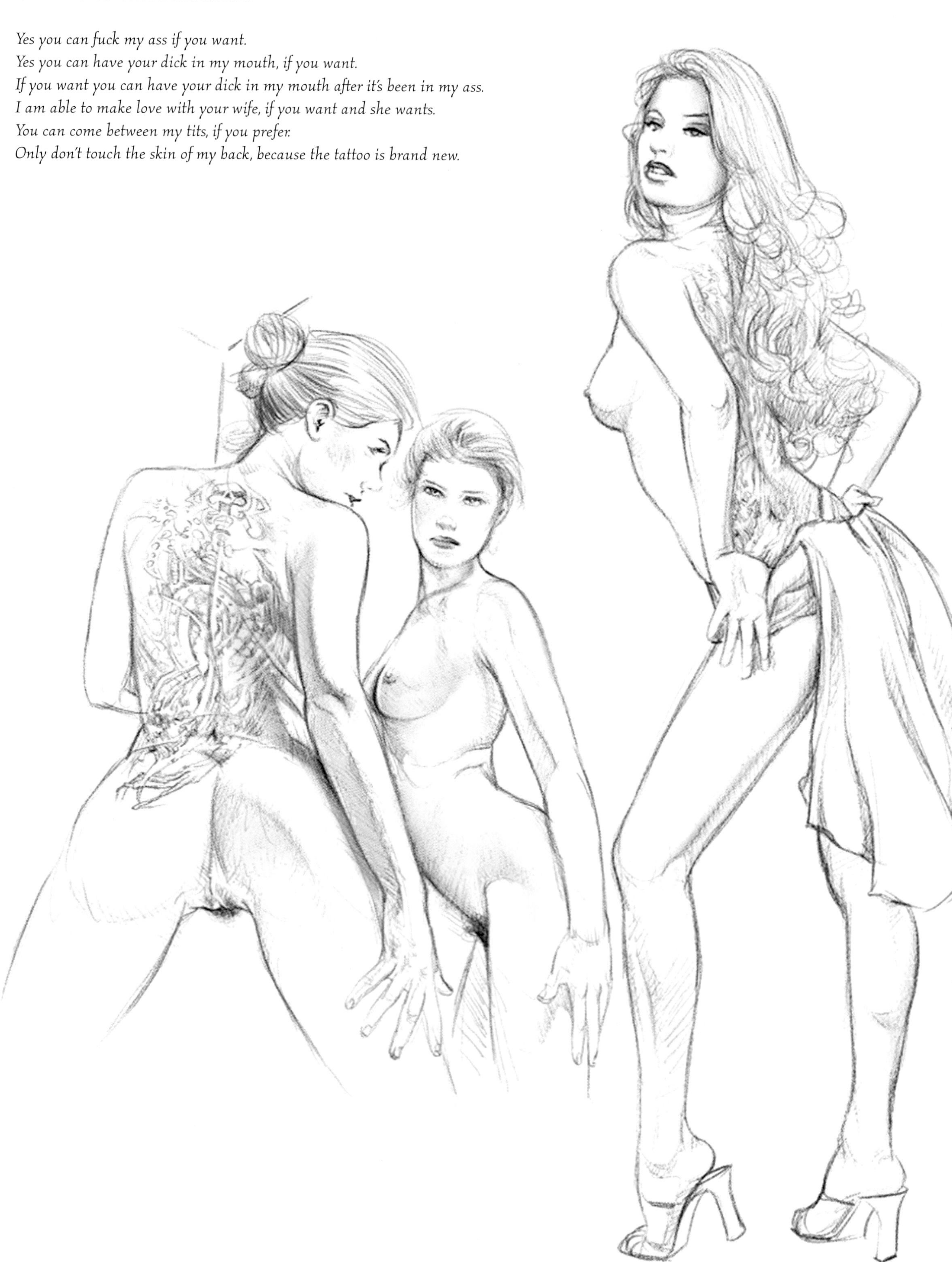

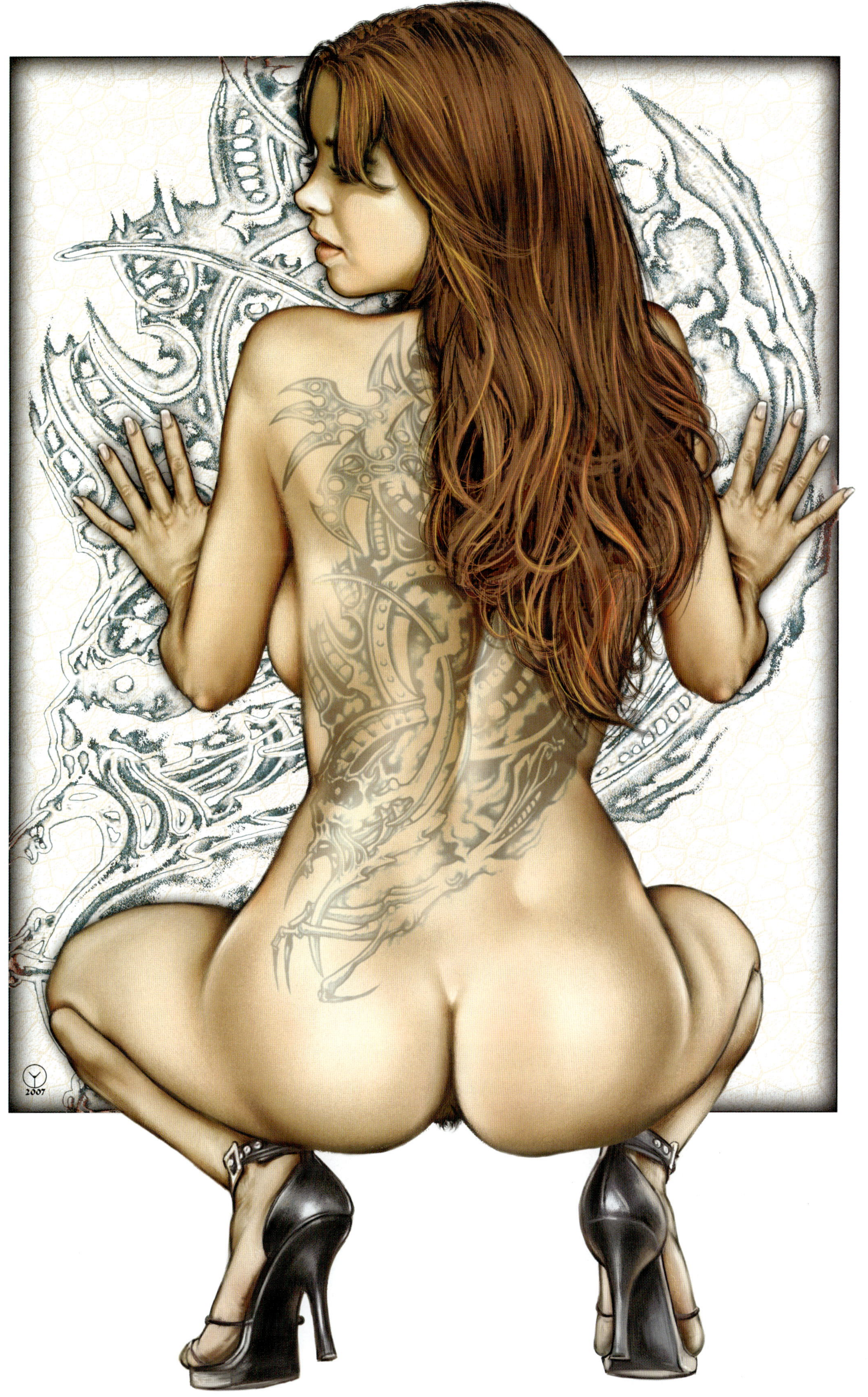
2007

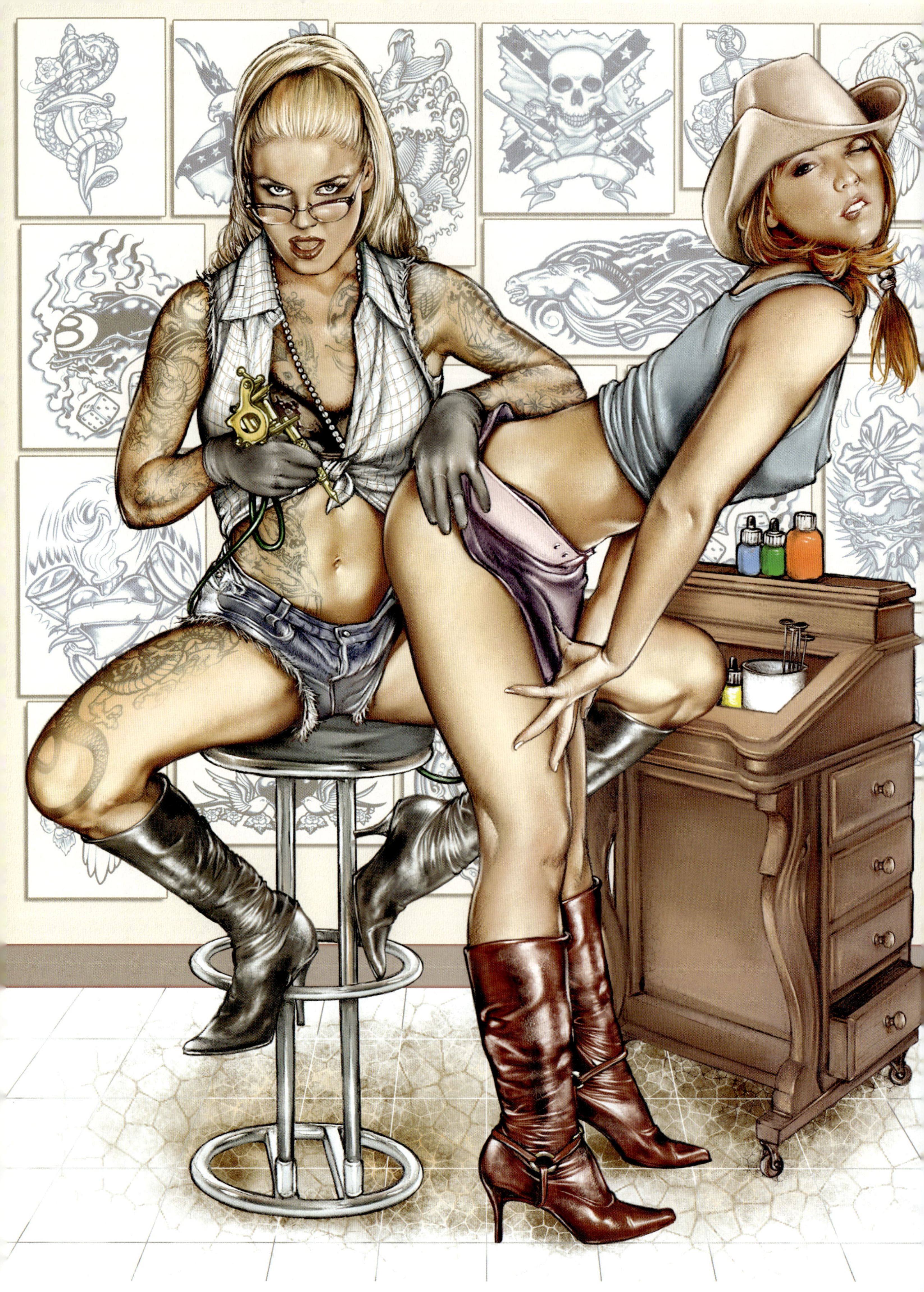